THE MISSION PLAN

THE COMPLETE GUIDE TO SUCCESS

Resources by Kyle S. King

The Mission Plan: The Decision

The Mission Plan: The Discovery

The Mission Plan: The Destiny

25 Years in Heaven: A Collection of Personal Poems

THE COMPLETE GUIDE TO SUCCESS

KYLE S. KING

Copyright © 2020 by Kyle S. King
All rights reserved. This book or any portion thereof
may not be reproduced or used in any manner whatsoever without the express written permission of the publisher except for the use of brief quotations in a book review.
Limits of Liability and Disclaimer of Warranty
The author and publisher shall not be liable for your misuse of this material. This book is strictly for informational and educational purposes. The purpose of this book is to educate and entertain. The author and/or publisher do not guarantee that anyone following these techniques, suggestions, tips, ideas, or strategies will become successful. The author and/or publisher shall have neither liability nor responsibility to anyone with respect to any loss or damage caused, or alleged to be caused, directly or indirectly by the information contained in this book.

Views expressed in this publication do not necessarily reflect the views of the publisher.

Printed in the United States of America

ISBN 978-1-948270-75-5

Keen Vision Publishing, LLC

www.keen-vision.com

"The meaning of life is to find your gift. The purpose of life is to give it away..."

Pablo Picasso

CONTENTS

A Letter To My Readers   9

SECTION ONE
The Mission Plan: The Decision
I Dedicate This to The World   21
Introduction: The King On The Hill   25
Chapter One: What's Your Net Worth?   47
Chapter Two: Become The Ceo Of You   61
Chapter Three: Divine Right Or Destiny   81
Chapter Four: Observe, Learn, & Grow   99
Chapter Five: Now, What's Stopping You?   123

SECTION TWO
The Mission Plan: The Discovery
Miracles   141
Introduction: Make A Difference   143
Chapter One: Mission Planning   159
Chapter Two: Sharpening Success Skills   175

Chapter Three: Teamwork Is Why The Dream Works   195
Chapter Four: 3…2…1… Jump!   205
Chapter Five: The Backseat Drivers   223

SECTION THREE
The Mission Plan: The Destiny

Let's Work   245
Introduction: Locker Room of Love   249
Chapter One: Pouring from an Empty Glass   265
Chapter Two: Eight Rounds of Success   281
Chapter Three: The Gold Medalist of Life   295
Chapter Four: The Fight, The Hike & The Light   311
Chapter Five: IPO: Welcome to the Life Market   323

About The Author   331
Stay Connected   333

A LETTER TO MY READERS

My Dear Friend,

Thank you. Your time is precious. You could be anywhere else, but I am thankful you are here with me. I'm honored that you picked up this book. And, whether you know it or not, you are supporting a childhood dream that with resilience, authenticity, and good work ethic became a reality. I will repay your kindness by promising that the time you spend reading this book will be beneficial, enriching, successful, and perhaps, even transformative. All this from a book? You bet.

Yehuda Berg once said, "Words have energy and power with the ability to help, to heal, to hinder, to hurt, to harm, to humiliate, and to humble." Like Yehuda Berg, I believe that words have power. If we speak words that are kind, loving, positive, uplifting, and encouraging, we can plant seeds into the earth that will one day sprout into a harvest that will change the world. And, who doesn't love to read? Through reading, we can disappear into untraveled worlds of fresh therapeutic experiences, far away from the hustle and bustle of our daily lives. If we go deep enough, the words on the pages will leap to life in our winds, and we will begin to see pictures through our imaginations that can enhance our experiences.

As far as I'm concerned, our love for reading makes us good friends already. The Mission Plan Mastery: A Complete Guide to Success is my keenest intent to grab you by the collar and haul you off to a faraway place where you have escaped your problems, overcome your trials and tribulations, and found strength in your insecurities. In this faraway place, I hope you are empowered to make better decisions, motivated to start working towards your dreams and inspired to make changes in your life so you can impact the lives of others once you return to reality. I truly believe that upon the stage that will be set throughout our journey, you will be inspired to produce the movie of your dreams, write the story of your imagination, and create the innovation for solving the world's problems.

I first experienced the transforming and freeing power of reading at a very young age. As I matured, I began to long for that getaway. My desires led me to experience many different books. Many of which, changed my life, actions, and beliefs. Some of them shaped the way I do business, while others transformed the way I do life. With so many good reads already available at your fingertips you may ask, "How will this book be different?" I'm going to place the keys you need to succeed right in the palm of your hands and show you what to do with them. I implore you not to just throw the keys on your coffee table or into that junk drawer in your kitchen. In-

A LETTER TO MY READERS

stead, find a nice keychain, hook them on, and keep them close by. Take these keys and begin to try them at every door of opportunity. As you use some of the keys, you will find that the door you are attempting to unlock will fly open immediately. However, other keys may require a little jiggling and shaking. But, if you are persistent, those doors will open unto you as well. Are you ready for your next set of keys? Well, I'm most certainly ready to hand them over to you.

I once read that a fool learns from his own mistakes, whereas a wise man learns from the mistakes of others. You're wise, and I was once a fool who made many mistakes. So, as you read, be sure to learn from them. On this journey, I will use the power of affirmations and transparency to enrich your life. Your life, at this present moment, reflects the words you have chosen to accept as the truth. More than anything, I desire that you will come to understand the dominion you've been granted over your reality. When you realize that you are the creator of your reality, you will regain power by speaking positive things into your life. This book will have a direct impact on your life and turn your negative feelings towards your mistakes into monuments of your success. The power of the words in this book and the words you will begin to use will drastically improve your quality of life. And before you know it, you will begin to live a life of true meaning and ultimate purpose.

Am I promising to make you successful? No, of course not. Only you can do that. Your success is already within you, but I do promise to show you how to access it so you can bring it out for the world to experience. During the course of your reading, I will outline many different strategies for feeding your focus and starving your distractions. I'll share recipes for brewing your tasty success stew. The success adventure may be rough, bumpy, or tough, but with a solid and attainable plan, you will be prepared to embrace every part of the ride. Before we begin, however, I have a few questions for you:

1. Have you ever felt like you were at a stop light in your life and it just never seemed to turn green?
2. Have you ever felt like you were making progress, but within moments, everything fell apart?
3. Have you ever wanted to do better, but didn't know what to do, when to start, how to begin, or where to go to get advice?

If you answered yes to any of the above questions, you are holding the right book. I've often been told that my wisdom, drive, and knowledge far surpass many within my age group. However, what many people don't know is that the failures, mistakes, and disappointments I've experienced played a major part in everything I know today.

Rachel Wolchin quoted, "It's not how we make mistakes, but how we correct them that defines us." It is those mistakes in life that allow us to develop into the individuals that lead others. I never look at making mistakes as a time for disappointment, but as a time to set a bridge for more opportunities to present in the future. It doesn't matter where you were, what trouble you got into, what failures you may have incurred, or mistakes you may have made, what you are doing now is what will bring light to a more promising future. So, stop sweating your past, and take action for a better future.

As an adult, I have learned that it is often when we experience our deepest disappointments that we come to realize our true purpose and full potential in life. The mistakes that cut us the deepest make us grateful for the knowledge we've gained through the growing and regenerative process. Sometimes, our biggest failures turn out to be not only our best opportunities to learn, but also the catalyst that now moves or motivates us to grow into the person we are meant to become.

For every time that you will want to give up, quit, or throw in the towel, I hope this letter will remind you why you can't give up. It is my hope that my story will be your double shot of espresso on those nights when you feel like you are too tired to go on.

This book is for the daughter who grew up without a father, the son who had no mother, or the man or woman who just needs some encouragement. This book is for those who may have been through some things and don't know what to do or where to go from their last mistake. I was that kid who made terrible decisions that could have cost me my life. I was that kid who lied, cheated, and stole just to fit in and be cool. I was the boy who learned from those mistakes, tough times, and times of desperation, and now, I'm the man who is changing the world. If it hadn't been for those obstacles, struggles, trials, and misfortunes, none of this would have been possible. Success didn't find me. I created it from the bridges of opportunities that I gained from the experiences of my failures.

The moment you stop fighting is the moment you lose. The moment you give up is the moment everyone gives up on you. The moment you stop believing is the moment you lose all you worked for, dreamed about, and all God has prepared for you in the future. Because of my many encounters that looked like failure, that little boy from Georgia died, and a man blossomed. I learned how to turn this mistake into a monument, and how to turn those trials into telescopes to remain focused on the future. I turned my tears and disappointments into decisions to be the best man I could be. I made up my mind that I would not let anyone ever dictate my destiny.

Failure is a mental weakness or state of mind that can bring on physical weakness, causing your body to shut down. My father taught me that it is not so much about how you start something as it is about how you finish. The last quarter in sports is about the same as the last semester in school or the last few weeks of an internship. It is how you finish the game, the work experience, or the school year that means the most and truly shows your strength and character. We all have great ideas, and wonderful plans of how to execute them, but when times get tough, things don't go our way, and the odds are stacked against us, that is when we truly see how strong, committed, and passionate we really are. The stoplight that had you stuck for a while was only a speedbump, and you just need a push to the other side. This book, **The Mission Plan Mastery: A Complete Guide to Success**, is that push.

When you decide you want to do better in your life that is the first stepping out of your circumstance and into your calling. If you want better, are tired of the same repetitive cycle, and desire to figure out your purpose, you have committed to reading a book that will help you do just that. It is time to seek a higher form of yourself. It is time to go beyond your ego, beyond your arrogance, and seek a thorough journey on enhancing your internal spiritual being. Within this book, you will learn the power of detaching yourself from the potential outcome. You will reach a point of self-discovery and enlightenment of self- realization.

Growing up, my parents would often give me books to read out loud. In my youth, I hated this form of cruel and unusual punishment. As a nine-year-old kid in the suburbs, I was more concerned with playing outside with my friends. As I grew older, I became intrigued with acquiring knowledge. Books became a bridge to personal development, and I became an avid reader and scholar. The more I began to read, the more I learned. The more I learned, the more I changed. Reading and living have similarities that are difficult to overlook. Every experience, day, situation, trial, and encounter in your life is all part of the best-selling novel you are writing every day. While it may be hard to believe that your life is a novel, you must allow this truth to set in. Even if your life is never penned, typed, and published, you are still writing out your story every day you are blessed to take a breath. Yes, my friend, you are the author. Everything that you go through sets the introduction, body, climax, and conclusion of the book you are writing daily.

There are points in our lives where we are caught between people, decisions, situations, or even choices. We describe these situations to our friends, counselors, mentors, and at times, our parents. We expect to receive advice or guidance that will lead to the climax or turning point in our lives. We are challenged every day as the protagonist at war with the antagonist who wants to defeat us, friends who don't believe in us, or parents who want to direct our dreams in the direction they think is best. These points are not meant to make us stop. Instead, they give us something to keep writing about. Additionally, they push us to read the lives of others more.

When one chapter of our lives ends, that doesn't mean we cannot write a better next chapter. One bad experience doesn't mean that life is over. A life well-lived consists of various experiences. Goals, philosophies, knowledge, and ideas will all appear as one thing but morph into something else as we learn from these various experiences. There will be many destinations, departures, and arrivals, but we must continue to stay on track of the mission and purpose of our novel of life.

As you are writing your next chapter, be sure not to flip back and read the chapter before or try to change history. Too many times, we walk forward with our eyes looking backward. Author and philosopher Joseph Campbell said, "It is not until the later stages of one's life that you look back and see that each experience has a symmetry and reason and fits perfectly into the fabric of your life." The law of constant change states that everything in life is in the process of becoming something else. Before we can set the foundations of manifestation in our lives, we must first understand there is no point of arrival; there is only a point where we prepare to immediately leave for another. We must embrace changing chapters in our lives instead of fighting it. At times, we must understand what we learned from the chapters prior to getting to the climax of our lives. Just because chapters one through three did not have the best endings doesn't mean we cannot finish the chapters. The climax of your story is the most important.

In life, a life-threatening illness, bankruptcy, termination of a job, or even a bad breakup calls for change and action. While these are all unpleasant and may be forced upon us, they open our eyes to the change we need for growth. Accepting and being open to change is vital as we unfold our lives and legacies.

Everyone has a purpose in life, no matter the environment or circumstances, everyone has a unique set of gifts or talents that serve an intricate part of the universe. Your story is not your own; it is a gift meant to be given away to the masses. The biggest challenge is being authentic and understanding the importance of your brand.

I don't know about you, but I'm excited to begin. I'll meet you in Section One of our journey.

SECTION ONE
THE DECISION

Pablo Picasso quoted, *"The meaning of life is to find your gift. The purpose of life is to give it away."* Everyone has a purpose in life, not matter the environment, no matter the circumstance of situations, everyone has a unique set of gifts or talents that serve an intricate part in the universe. Your story is not your own, it is a gift meaning to be given away to the masses. The biggest challenge is being authentic and understanding the importance of your brand. During this section, you will learn how to release all the grief, heartbreak, and pain on your platform towards purpose. It is time for you to live your life as a miraculous expression of divinity not just on occasions, but in every moment, in every breath, and every step moving forward in your life. When your actions and passions align it moves into purposeful destiny. Through stories, examples and exercises, you'll be taught how expressing your unique talents and will ultimate lead to fulfilling the needs of the world whenever you want it. The very purpose of our lives is to seek happiness. This section will equip you with the tools to becoming carefree, joyful, happy and your life becomes an expression of unparalleled love and happiness.

I DEDICATE THIS TO THE WORLD

We're living in an information age
Where technology rules our thoughts
And machines control our days.
The hurtful truth about information
Is that it creates speculation
Instead of facts thoroughly thought out through education.
They don't teach us about theoretical education
Instead, we are taught to be entrepreneurial employees through employment and innovation.
But this mindset that has been created
Stems from a capitalist mindset
Indoctrinated into our minds, spirits, and even into our races.
Now economic gaps, lack of resources, and gentrification rule our nation.

But what is information?
It's nothing but speculation, thoughts, opinions, and man's definition of media content or declaration.
It is a limitless pill that keeps us limited from our human nature.
What does it mean to have free thought and to be the Michelangelo of our own portrait or painting?
To be the Leonardo da Vinci or Einstein, the original creator
Or would he be known as the primal failure?

THE MISSION PLAN: THE DECISION

Looking at the Oprah Winfrey's, Michael Jordan's, or even a historical figure such as an Angela Davis

There is power in resilience, education, and uniting with our neighbor.
Regardless of your color, race, gender, or ethnicity
You are worth more than wealth and your job on earth is more than a salary.
It's bigger than that investment portfolio, 401K Plan or what they decided to pay you hourly.

This book is dedicated to you, the dreamer, the believer, the critical thinker.
This book is dedicated to you, the single mother and the single father
And you, the brother or sister left by parents and forced to be a provider.
This book is dedicated to you; young girl and boy keep working hard
Regardless of what society has told you, reading these words means you've already come so far.

This book is for the older couple that lost their way
This book is for the retired veteran that needs something to make his or her day.
In a world filled with violence, hatred, and societal stereotypes
I dedicate this book to the generational cycles getting ready to be broken
The goals to be set and the preparation for long nights.

I DEDICATE THIS TO THE WORLD

Let your thoughts become focused
Let your dreams become true
Because everything you need is already inside of you.

"Your beliefs become your thoughts, your thoughts become your words, your words become your actions, your actions become your habits, your habits become your values, your values become your destiny."

– Mahatma Gandhi

INTRODUCTION
KING OF THE HILL

Every book is designed to create a personal dialogue between the writer and the individual reading it. Depending on who we are and what information we're looking for, we all have different reasons for picking up a book. Some read books in search of guidance or advise. Others use books as a basis for research on a specific topic of study. Many read simply to escape the everyday challenges of life. Growing up, I loved the Magic Treehouse book series. They kept my imagination active and at times, served as a getaway from life. I used those books to imagine leaving the country and exploring the world. Each book served a different purpose and gave me the opportunity to learn about the past, understand the present, and explore the future. I learned about different places around the world, and through each book, I picked up many new skills – problem-solving, in particular. These books changed my life by helping me connect with different cultures, places, experiences, and characters. Through the fiction stories I read, I created my own reality.

Since my days of Magic Treehouse, I've always been an avid reader. From reading poetry, Greek philosophy, self-development books, and at times, science fiction and fantasy novels, I learned many valuable lessons in some way, shape, or form. Each of these experiences has played an essential part in shaping me into the man I have become and preparing me for the vital role I will continue to grow into as I mature. In the many books I have read, I take stock of myself and analyze my mistakes through literature. This allows me to set a firm foundation for a balanced life. I have compiled my stories and combined them with the experiences of prominent professionals. I have refined those ideas to help others develop insights that will empower them to make necessary changes for a brighter future and an improved reality.

Many of us don't understand how to live within our reality because we are so focused on the dream of living within society. We are often measured by our accomplishments, success, and what we have earned. Imagine what life would be like if we were measured based on who we were and our character traits such as humility, integrity, and grace. Would the world be a better place? Or, would it be uncomfortable to have a world full of smiles, respect, and peace? Perhaps I've read too many Magic Tree House books, and the possibility to learn the power of meditation and examining one's own mental and emotional processes to develop character instead of being driven by capital is unrealistic.

The act of socialism, the development of classism, and the use of cultural or social racism within our society blinds us of the true beauty of human nature. No one should be looked down upon because of the street they grew up on, the ethnicity they are associated with, or the family they were born into. Many of this generation are bound by mental chains, blinded by monetary gain and financial fame, and have forgotten that it is the love of family and the positive empowerment of the people we care about that truly represent our own personal and professional success. None of us were born perfect, however, we must embrace each other's imperfection, work together, leverage each other's knowledge, and build a better world for all.

The definitions of accomplishment and success, in my opinion, are used to divide and disunite. Instead of unification, because of traits, culture, and character, our connections are based upon our accomplishments, the schools we graduate from, country clubs we are a part of, and even the economic classes we are classified into because of our tax brackets. This misconception of connection and the development of relationships leaves people emotionally ignorant to the purpose and primary function of life. The societal drive of accomplishments creates the powerful "C" word known as comparison. Against our self-interest, we get bogged down by shyness, self-consciousness, cynicism, pride, competitiveness, jealousy, and arrogance. Research conducted by Matthew Lieberman at UCLA shows that being social and connecting with others is a fundamental human need just as food, shelter, and water. Lieberman went on to discuss that we feel social pain, such as the loss of a relationship, in the same part of the brain that we feel physical pain. Social connection is not only important; it is a fundamental human need.

I am writing this book because it is important to me to

communicate and connect with as many people as humanly possible from a variety of backgrounds to influence positive change in the lives of others, even though we may never personally meet. I recognized at a very early age that it is my passion to add value to the lives of others, through whatever means I have available: my knowledge, life experiences, and/or wisdom I have gained in my time on earth. Through these experiences, I believe the greatest reward one can have in life is the sacrifice made on behalf of others that ultimately leads to an improvement in the quality of their lives – whether that sacrifice is in time, resources, or just succeeds in making someone's life more comfortable. Adding value to other people's lives is what I believe God placed me on this earth to do.

Within the critical state of our world, the only constant in life is change; without change, it is impossible to grow. Many people want change, but are afraid of it at the same time; therefore, many remain complacent. Complacency is a curse that inhibits otherwise intelligent men and women from fully reaching their potential.

The journey towards success is not a race or a sprint; it will not happen overnight. The journey towards success is a marathon that will take preparation, stamina, and many long days and nights. We all love a positive outcome, but we sometimes don't appreciate the process until the very end. Global philanthropist and one of the most successful businessmen of all time, Warren Buffet, quoted, "Someone is sitting in the shade today because someone planted a tree a long time ago." Success doesn't happen overnight, however, we must remember that the seeds we plant, water, and maintain every day will eventually become the harvest that catapults us into a successful future.

Success is a patient process; it is a practice of constant performance. One night, I watched a late night special on ESPN about Allyson Felix, a 9-time Olympic Medalist, 11-time world champion, and the most decorated Women's Track & Field Athlete of all time. She described how she hated every minute of training, but when she won her first Olympic Gold Medal, the indescribable feeling she experienced at that moment made all the hard work worth it. She went on to talk about how grateful she was for her coaches and their training; so much so, she began to work even harder. Her renewed diligence made her even faster, stronger, and more mentally focused. In fact, she became so fast, that she set and broke her records and went on to win five more Olympic Gold Medals.

Was her success attributed to talent, hard work, a gift, or just luck? The real question here is: What is talent, anyway? According to Webster, the definition of talent is "any natural ability or power." I have a different theory. I don't believe in talent, I believe in obsession, knowledge, and excellence. You can be anyone you want to be if you put in the time, invest the resources, and give the effort to whatever you want to become. The greatest have mastered an obsession to be great at what they were interested in doing. They consistently worked on their interest and over time, it became an implied learned behavior – their actions became a part of their cognitive processing.

Behavior derived from knowledge and skills can be changed far more easily than talent-based behavior. Knowledge and skilled-based behaviors allow you to develop the power of critical thought and problem-solving instead of environmental ignorance and the inability to cast your net outside of your state of mind. No matter our profession, lane, or the hat we wear, we are all introduced to ideas, knowledge, and valuable information in our everyday lives that, through our personal experiences, act as tools for our toolkit when we are building the trajectory of our lives. There is always something to learn or gain from each experience we face as humans – whether positive or negative.

Albert Einstein said, "The definition of insanity is doing the same thing over and over and expecting different results." I believe the same concept can apply to ignorance. One definition of ignorance is having a negative experience in life, learning a harmful or unfavorable lesson from that experience, and then either consciously or unconsciously choosing to repeat behaviors that guarantee that the negative experience will repeat in ones' life. Ignorance may resemble the following scenario.

A girl grows up in an environment where her father, although loving to her, is chronically unfaithful to her mother. She witnesses her mother's pain and anxiety and loses respect for her as she forgives her husband repeatedly for the same offense. When the young girl becomes a woman, she commits herself to a young man very much like her father. She continuously catches her boyfriend cheating on her, but she too continuously forgives his infidelity; she prays that he changes his behavior. She complains to her friends and seeks advice from others. She believes the same lies, excuses, and promises in which she grew up hearing her father make to her mother. She considers the mirror and hardly recognizes the woman gazing back at her. No matter what anyone does or says, she stays and continues to try and fix an unfixable situation.

Just in case this one did not resonate with you, let's take a look at a more tangible scenario of a man who has revolutionized the technological era of the 20th century, built a multi-billion dollar business when no one believed that his idea was great enough, was fired and casted out from his own company, returned to that same company years later to grow the company larger than any other company in the world, took one idea, and continued to work on it repeatedly until he found the results in which he searched for. This man didn't stop until his dream was his reality. This man is known to many as Steve Jobs, but to some, he is known as the God Father of Technology. Before Mr. Jobs passed away in 2011, he quoted, "Here's to the crazy ones, the misfits, the rebels, the troublemakers, the round pegs in the square holes... the ones who see things differently – they're not fond of rules... You can quote them, disagree with them, glorify or vilify them, but the only thing you can't do is ignore them because they change things. They push humans forward, and while some may see them as the crazy ones, we see genius, because the ones who are crazy enough to think that they can change the world, are the ones who do."

We are not faced with moments like these very often, but when we are called upon to make a choice, take a stance, grasp the lesson, learn from it, and move on, that is what we must do. This is not the time to pick it up, brush it off yet again and start right back at square one or fall back into the same trap we previously left. This moment is either a character builder or a character breaker.

As I sit here and reminisce about my current state, it is not the mistakes of others that got me $20,000 in debt. It is not the mistakes of others that got two women pregnant within a year's time. It is not the mistakes of others that got me into this state of disbelief and struggle. I chose credit over cash. I chose my flesh over the instructions of Christ. My choices and my mistakes landed me where I am. Hal Elrod once quoted, "The moment you take responsibility for everything in your life is the moment you can change anything in your life." This quote proved to be very true for me, as it will be for you.

Growing up, my father admonished me to be humble. "You got to be humble, Kyle. You have to be humble. Stop being so arrogant. Stop being so cocky. Yes, you can be confident, but you still have to be humble," he would often remind me. I never thought that you could essentially be confident like the Tom Brady's, The Kobe Bryant's, The LeBron James's, or even the Barack Obama's and still have humility. It wasn't until I was listened to my pastor explain that you must go through the humiliation process to learn how to be truly humble that I learned how to be confidently humble. A lot of times, we are told to do something or be something, but never told how to go about it. We learn, as time progresses, that the process of learning how comes as we attempt to be. How do we go about being humble? How do we become successful? How do we become confident? How do we let go of our fears and insecurities? How do we truly become the person we want to become? We are never given the instructions on how to do it. We are never given the guide or that manual on how to do something. The knowledge we have is from our experiences, or, in most cases, we are a product of our environments or circumstances.

When I first had my son, everyone told me to be a good father and a good man. Each time I was given this advice, I often wondered, but how? How do I go about being a good father, and who determines what is a good father versus a bad father? I always thought that everything in life came with a how-to guide. When you buy something for your home, there are steps and tools in the box to help you assemble your purchase. The bittersweet thing about life is that there's never been, nor will there ever be, a how-to guide to become the best version of you. Everyone is unique in their own way. Everyone is packaged differently and will assemble to be something different in life.

What works for most may not work for you. What didn't work for many may be the step that activates your success. When we look at being successful, humble, or financially free, the how-to guide is within us, within our experiences, and within the lessons we learned from other people. Every experience is a new chapter in our book of destiny. To truly become the success we desire to be, we must learn to look at the disappointments of life as lessons instead of loss.

On April 10, 2015, I stood on the rooftop of the InterContinental Hotel in downtown Atlanta, Georgia. My body was weak; I was in pain. My pockets were empty from my attempt to chase the fame. Tears constantly filled my eyes and gave way to my cheeks. My chest hurt from the cold air that I exhaled deeply; but, it was nothing like the pain I felt in my heart. Close friends had turned their backs on me and colleagues had stolen my dreams. However, in my moment of despair, I realized that through all I had faced, I could still stand strong and believe. American entrepreneur, businessman, inventor, and industrial designer Steve Jobs said a powerful quote before his death in 2011, "If you haven't found it yet, keep looking." Steve Jobs, also known as the creator of Apple, Inc., couldn't find the initial seed money to start, at the time, just a tech company in a garage, but he kept looking. He never settled. As a result, he revolutionized technology and created the now leader in technology and world innovation, Apple, Inc.

No matter how hard life may seem, no man can place a value on you or your destiny; God has already finished your dream. Continue to walk forward. Trust in Him, learn from your mistakes, and continue to grow. I assure you, life is a learning process, and the state you're in is the beginning of your life lesson — not the end.

The Mission Plan Series is designed to teach you how to overcome obstacles and not allow your current environment, situation, or circumstance define your identity and destiny. In a system built off our socioeconomic status, at times, people don't believe there is an abundance of opportunity to be taken advantage of if one was not born with a silver spoon in his or her mouth. However, this book points the finger back at you and challenges you to learn from your experiences to become uniquely and distinctly great in whatever you choose to do. This book will cover many different topics and provide transferable skills that will elevate your life and set a solid foundation upon which you can build your personal and professional success.

Continue to read this book as I take life lessons from all facets of life, whether business, education, religion, or my personal experiences and deliver them with transparency and authenticity. I hope that this will be the first of many books that I will write to help you as you pursue your leadership and professional goals. This information has already radically changed the lives of many and has the potential to change your life as well.

My family's lack of resources growing up, the lack of opportunity, and challenges I faced on this journey did not dictate my success but may have prevented me from failure. There is a popular saying, "The only way I can go is up because things can't get any worse." An abundance of opportunity, money, and resources was not my recipe for success, and it sure as hell isn't the recipe for yours. It doesn't take large investments, Ivy League Schools, and a closet filled with nice, expensive clothes to be successful. The late, great coach of the Los Angeles Lakers, Phil Jackson, said it best about Kobe Bryant after a big win. He stated, "Kobe just has the will to win and he doesn't accept losing or failure." Anything besides a WILL is an accessory, a distraction, and blockage that blinds you from the true work that it takes for you to be successful.

We hear a lot of success stories about people who started from the bottom, worked hard, and eventually became successful. We hear other stories about people whose parents gifted them the money they needed to start a company or those who received money using an inheritance, were born into wealth or privy to inside knowledge on how to leverage the current system. We don't hear too many stories about the kids in the middle who witnessed two hard-working parents who provided for their family and how those kids learned valuable skills and lessons and turned that work ethic into successful entrepreneurship.

So, let me tell you my story. It is a little different than most of the stories I have read about. I grew up as that middle-class kid raised with both of my biological parents and a strong support system around me that proved to be a competitive advantage going into the marketplace of life. Neither one of my parents went to college; they barely made it through high school. They grew up in the inner-city projects of South Jersey, and neither of them had parental or family support to back their dreams. I would always ask them what their dreams were growing up, and the only response both my mother and father would give me was to make it out of the "hood" and grant their children with a better life than they had. My parents have been married for over 25 years, own two homes, together make over $200,000 annually, have raised three children who all went to college, and are positioning themselves to own another investment property. My father instilled good values and morals and aided in the development of my character. He taught me the importance of social inheritance instead of just being able to inherit real estate and wealth. He taught me the importance of my legacy and my character. He taught me to see the value in passing down lessons to my children instead of just investments. Warren Buffet said it best about the idea of inheritance, "A very rich person should leave his kids enough to do anything but not enough to do nothing." As part of the generation of activists, my desire to leave a philanthropic legacy compared to a professional legacy was birthed from the teachings of my father.

My mother empowered the inner entrepreneur inside of me. She fired up the warrior who continued to fight no matter the circumstance. The teachings and experiences I learned from my mother as a child ultimately taught me never to let the sounds of the audience affect my performance during the game. To put their parenting style simply, my father taught me how to serve, and my mother taught how to earn. When I was about thirteen years old, I asked my parents for money or "an allowance" as the other kids would call it. My father had a thing for comparing my questions to when he was my age to make me think, so he replied, "I couldn't ask my mother for anything because she didn't have anything to give." My mother, on the other hand, always left me with an answer that motivated me to take action, she replied, "If you want it, you have to work for it, boy. Nothing is given around here; everything you want is earned."

From that day forward, I began my transformation into the businessman I am today. Every thought that flowed through my brain was about how I could turn my ideas it into a profitable company. A wise man once told me, "Don't ever belittle your dreams because if you start to do that, you will be finished." I became a year-round entrepreneur at the age of 14. When I say year-round, I mean year-round. In the spring, I washed the neighbors' cars every day. I asked them to supply the water hose, and I brought everything else. In the summer, I cut grass, pulled weeds out of the ground, and organized peoples' homes. In the fall, I raked leaves in the yards in the neighborhood and charged everyone the same price. In the winter, I shoveled snow out of driveways and off cars. While some kids were only willing to make money during sunny days or cool winter nights, I offered services for every season and weather condition, and I was willing to do more for less.

THE MISSION PLAN: THE DECISION

I was able to earn income year-round. Through my various entrepreneurial endeavors, I learned the importance of diversifying my portfolio and not keeping all my eggs in one basket. My concept was very similar to the business model of Amazon or Walmart. I aimed to work directly with the suppliers and provide quality services at an affordable price to serve everyone instead of a certain target market. This made me different from the competition because I believed that I would make the same exact amount as those charging more for larger lawns. What I didn't make in pricing, I made in sheer volume. This concept taught me the idea of having a competitive advantage.

Those year-round side hustles brought in about $500.00 per week. I did it so cheaply because my father always taught me, "Be of service and bring value to others. It is okay not to make as much. If you are doing something well enough, you will eventually make your money. Be patient, and it will come to you."

You know, it's funny. Even though I had a lot of entrepreneurial side hustles growing up, I never dreamed of becoming an entrepreneur or business owner. My goal was to become a medical doctor. As a kid, I thought medicine was the only profession that could truly make a difference in people's lives. In college, however, I discovered that it wasn't about the external profession; it was about the internal passion that birthed purpose.

My organization, Project SHINE, Inc., is a non-profit organization headquartered in Huntsville, Alabama. It is an educational initiative geared to cultivating underrepresented students into globally competitive business leaders. In the beginning stages of establishing Project SHINE, Inc., a past negative perception of me heavily impacted the success my project. I had to improve that perception to ensure the future success and expansion of the brand. In business and life, a person's perception of you and your work is critical to the stability and sustainability of whatever endeavor you are associated with.

At Project SHINE, we focus on training and equipping students by providing them with the necessary skills and resources to be successful business professionals. We've learned that one of the biggest problems this next generation faces is that the students are not mentally, physically, emotionally, intellectually, or professionally prepared to go into the workforce and perform. We must understand that education goes further than what is taught through lectures in the classroom. Education is being able to apply what is learned and critically think of creative solutions to solve the problems we are facing today; whether those problems are in business, economics, politics, or just in life. Education, according to Albert Einstein, is what remains after one has forgotten what one has learned in school. Education is about filling the many gaps in our society; the gaps between the economically poor and the financially free, gaps between salaries of men and women, and even the gaps between business and academia.

Project SHINE birthed out of the idea that by advancing underrepresented students through a comprehensive educational process, we could promote excellence and provide them with those specific skills necessary to become globally competitive business leaders. Education is the foundation of our very existence, so this initiative provides a pathway to economic growth by serving, educating, empowering, and developing students by using educational excellence as a pipeline to personal and professional success.

This company was founded upon the foundation of making a difference and not being so focused on making dollars. Making money is still important, however, how we value the bottom line of this organization is by the change we make in the world through improving, innovating, impacting, and inspiring the next generation of future leaders. Through educational enrichment programs, seminars, coaching programs, personal and professional development workshops, and sharing knowledge, we focus on empowering the next generation of future business leaders.

In the beginning, I built a strong team that would contribute to the long-term sustainability of the organization. One day, I received a phone call from my assistant director of marketing and planning. I knew it was a serious matter because it was around 11:45 PM when I got the call. She articulated that if we were planning on working together, I had to ensure that whatever I used to be, whatever reputation I used to have, whatever I used to do, and however I used to act was finished because her brand was associated with either the success or failure of the organization. At the first sound of hearing these words, I was disappointed that my past actions had influenced the current situation as we planted the seeds for the future. Additionally, I was also taken aback because no one had ever been so direct and transparent with me about who I was and how that could potentially impact my future success.

This brings me to a strong point about your brand, image,

and the overall perception others have of you. Though we hate to admit it, the world's perception of you matters. This fact was made real to me during my study of Daymond John's book, The Power of Broke. In the book, he explains how what you do, what you wear, what you say, who you associate yourself with, who you sleep with, etc. is a direct reflection of who you are. You are what you do, and you will only go as far as the world allows you. On the one hand, I was just trying to build an organization and bring the right people on board to help me run the business. On the other hand, the energy I had already put into the world was negatively affecting the image of the brand and could have negatively impacted the success of the organization.

I want you to understand the importance of aligning your values with your dreams, aligning your passion with the perception, and aligning who you are in private to what the public eye thinks of you. You cannot and will not be successful if you are not walking, talking, eating, and training your mind to be consistently successful. I know it is very cliché, but what you put in is what you will get out. Furthermore, what you put out, is what will come back to you.

As a teenager, I chased women and got into trouble with my friends, but because I wasn't caught by any adults back then, I thought that I was free and clear and could live happily ever after. Life isn't a fairy tale, and this isn't the Disney Channel; things don't always work out as we think they will. Some of our mistakes aren't as easily forgotten as changing the channel on the television. Those same bad habits that I cultivated in high school firmly implanted in my mind and impacted the energy I put out into the world. The same lies

THE MISSION PLAN: THE DECISION

I used to get what I wanted were still very much a part of my present. My behavior and thought processes forced me to transfer from my first university. I was harassed, labeled, and placed into a situation where my life was threatened, all because I attempted to beat the system.

If you want success, become the success you wish to have by first transforming your mind. Many long to live a luxurious lifestyle, but feed their minds with minimum wage level knowledge. Others dream of being wealthy, but their minds are stuck in poverty-stricken thinking. Successful people emulate and learn from other successful people. What are you currently reading or doing that can add to your success? Instagram posts, Snapchat videos, nor your strong desire to impress someone will get you any closer to your goals or contribute to your success. Successful people think, talk, and approach life differently; they do what a majority of people don't.

In 2015, I gave a speech to a stadium full of high school students. I stated that if you are the smartest, strongest, fastest, most motivated person in your group, team, or "clique," it's time to find a new crew. I expressed to them that friends who allow them to be complacent will waste their time instead of challenging them to be successful. Your continued success depends on who you hang with, what you listen to, what you eat, what you read, how and where you spend your time, and how you think. You must envision the change you want and then be that change. Every day you wake up, go to work, play that sport, draw that painting, or rap that lyric to the best of your ability. During my undergraduate years at Alabama A&M University, I wore a suit to class every single day my last year of college. Every single day I was ostracized, talked about negatively, and laughed at by the fans in the stands. However, I wasn't focused on what was going on in the stadium; I knew what I was trying to accomplish on the court of my calling. I knew I wanted to be a successful businessman, and at the time, I was in the beginning stage of building my first successful business, Project SHINE. I maxed out two credit cards and bought suits, socks, shoes, briefcases, and everything businessmen had that made them look like they do. I went to Barnes and Noble's and bought two books a month on business, personal, and professional development and brand development. I took that knowledge and put it into practice in my life. I talked, walked, ate, and looked like a businessman. What did I become by the second semester before I graduated college? A successful businessman with a blossoming non-profit organization.

THE MISSION PLAN: THE DECISION

For this challenge, you will need one sheet of paper and something to write with. Draw a line across the middle of the paper horizontally. Then, draw a line to separate the top half of the paper. This should split the paper in to four blocks.

INSTRUCTIONS

1. In block one, write down what you are good at.
2. In block two, write down what makes you happy.
3. In block three, write down your daily routine.
4. In block four, review your blocks. Write done what you are doing that does not correlate with your strengths and your happiness.
5. Flip the paper over, write down small changes you can make to do better, be better, and live better!

TIPS FOR SUCCESS

Stop wasting your time. Improve your strengths. Stop expecting others to make you happy and stop blaming your unhappiness on other people. 95% of the time, your happiness weighs heavily on something that you are either doing or not doing.

Every day could potentially be your last. Focus on activities that add to your happiness, bettering your strengths, and increasing your success.

Only engage in activities that bring your mind, body, and spirit value. Throw the rest in the trash.

"Our success has a direct correlation to our work ethic. Our work has a direct correlation with our knowledge. Our knowledge has a direct correlation with our experiences. Our experiences are directly correlated with our involvement and exposure."

-Kyle Scott King, Author and Entrepreneur

CHAPTER ONE
WHAT'S YOUR NET WORTH?

Since I was young, my mother always told me, "Your network defines your net worth." I never understood her statement until I was a sophomore in college. She would often explain how she leveraged contacts and positioned herself to be the first and only black female senior executive for Volvo Cars of North America. My mother was an unorthodox candidate for this job because she lacked a college education and any formal education past high school. But one thing I have observed about my mother is that she has a very engaging and winning personality. She is the ultimate people person, and she understands what makes others tick. My mother is a master at "playing the game" in business. Before my sophomore year in college, I didn't understand how my network of people, resources, and contacts could have any correlation with how much money I was worth. I didn't see how who I was connected to or who liked me could transfer into real capital. I continued to observe her interactions when she took me to corporate events or gatherings with her colleagues. Not only did my mother have a very extensive network of associates, she understood people and how to connect with them on the most personal level by building relationships.

When people ask me for one piece of advice I would give to students, I say, "Gain as much experience and exposure as you can." I believe experience and exposure is the biggest gap between the economically poor and the financially free. Those ten percenters were exposed early on to different ideas, perspectives, business opportunities, knowledge, and circles. Their sphere of influence is different than the average joe. They are a part of different clubs, activities, social and professional groups, and think tanks. All of these different experiences and interactions provided them with the exposure needed to understand what is going on the world, paint a different picture, and learn how to create the solutions for the problems that the majority of people are facing. It is not all about the education. Education is universal, we are all learning the same things, and 2 + 2 is four anywhere in the world. However, the difference is how you apply knowledge. We learn how to best apply knowledge by gaining experience and exposure.

Expose yourself to different professions and activities. Travel to different cities and expose yourself to different ways of living and cultures. Meet different people and learn new knowledge. Take up a new hobby or apply for an internship outside of your field or major. The highest performing professionals are those who can understand different perspectives and leverage their knowledge in a way that will create solutions for their problems. It doesn't matter how much education you have obtained; experience and application are the best and only teacher. How do you create value as a manager if you don't understand the processes at the entry level? How do you make a sound decision as a CFO for your dealerships in the automotive industry if you have never stepped foot in one? Until you go out and work in the school system, your master's in education won't mean anything. Until you go out and do your first auditing report, that degree in accounting won't mean anything. Until you begin your first day as president, all of those plans you talked about during your campaign won't mean a thing. To perfect your craft, you have to gain experience. Become comfortable with being uncomfortable, and you will begin to realize your true passions and purpose in life. When people expose themselves to different people, experiences, and perspectives, I believe it truly sets the foundation towards success.

In my first year of college, I tried to do what my mother did. I skated through class and didn't work hard. I made it a point to meet influential people and build those personal relationships with them. At the end of my freshman year of college, I had a 2.21 GPA and some of the trouble that I had gotten myself into trying to "connect," caused me to wind up transferring universities. When I transferred, I took this as an opportunity to start fresh and focus on myself and my education. I separated myself from the rest of the student body for the first semester of school and ended the semester with a 4.0, earning A's in all my courses. It was then that I was invited to executive box seats at football games and private luncheons. I was introduced to influential people because of my work ethic and focus in the classroom. I was so focused, that I brought my book bag to the football games; I'm not kidding. During breaks or halftime, I studied my lessons and took notes. I instantly became a leader among my peers and built a strong professional network. Because of these experiences I finally understood my mother's statement and even added an important variable to her wise equation.

YOUR NETWORK + YOUR WORK ETHIC = YOUR NET WORTH

Many think net worth only has a financial connotation and that is a major misconception. The word net, and not the internet, simply means total after expenses. So, if you have a product that you sold for $100 but it took you $50 to make it, then your NET earnings is $50. Worth is defined as an amount of something that has a specified value, that lasts for a specified length of time. Worth is not just measured by money. Sometimes, the connections you make, experiences you are exposed to, and encounters you have are worth much more than any dollar amount.

The power of your network can truly enhance your net worth. The more people you are connected to gives you the opportunity of gaining more knowledge, skills, insight, and value across the board. Your connections allow you to gain access to information that wasn't available to you without your connections. This makes YOU more valuable and increases your WORTH. The more, or the total amount of people that you are connected to, and information that you gain, makes the net of the worth wider and increases your overall net worth.

But here is the catch: What are you bringing to the table? What value do you bring? What can you offer someone? How do you ensure that your relationships are mutually beneficial? The best relationships in any industry are those that benefit everyone involved. This is why I added the variable "work ethic" to my mother's equation. Without good work ethic, you won't add value to others who are successful, and they are less likely to allow you access into their circles.

DEFINE YOUR DASH

Before the New Year, people take the time to write a long list, full of "resolutions," action plans, and goals they hope to accomplish the next year. The new year resolution conversations typically surface somewhere around November, with two months still left in the year to begin making a difference, but I digress. Some people take these lists seriously, however, majority are committed for the first few months and then fall off the wagon and go right back to their old habits. But, why? Why don't our actions align with our commitments? Why doesn't our individual worth align with the wealth we want to gain from other people? Inconsistency? Yes. Procrastination? That's another great answer. Pure Laziness? Yes, even laziness. However, I implore you to look deeper. Why do we allow inconsistency, procrastination, and laziness to diminish our work ethic? Because we have yet to define our dash.

THE MISSION PLAN: THE DECISION

Let's take a look at the tombstone inscription of one of the most influential leaders in the Civil Rights Movement, Dr. Martin Luther King, Jr.

REV. MARTIN LUTHER KING, JR.
(1929-1968)
"Free at last. Free at last. Thank God Almighty I'm Free at last."

Upon this tombstone located at the Martin Luther King, Jr National Historic Site in Atlanta, GA lies something very significant. It's not his title, or the quote from one of his most historical and celebrated speeches. Instead, it is something that can be found on every tombstone. It is located right between the year of birth and the year of death. It is the dash. That dash encapsulates so much and speaks to your whole life. Your dash is what will empower the eulogy and final remarks spoken over your body. The dash represents everything you did from the moment you opened your eyes for the first time to the moment you closed your eyes for the last time. It speaks about who you are, who you helped, what you did, and what you accomplished. Whether your dash will represent something positive or negative depends heavily upon how you define it now. Define your dash by asking yourself questions like:

What do I want to be remembered for?
What do I want my legacy to be?
Do I even want to be remembered?

In one of my favorite movies, Gladiator, before he led his cavalry into battle, Gladiator Maximus Decimus Meridius says, "What we do in life echoes in eternity." Every decision we make in life has a positive or negative outcome that we will be remembered for. After you define your dash, begin to analyze how and where you spend your time, your eating and sleeping habits, and your work ethic. Will your current way of life lead to how you desire to be remembered when you die?

TIME MANAGEMENT

We cannot change anything in history, nor can we can cure anything that is currently taking place However, we can problem solve to prevent negative things from taking place in our future. Just take a look at the medical research. There are many diseases we cannot cure, like cancer. Though we cannot cure cancer presently, doctors and scientists can create a preventative that will lower development of cancer around the country. Yes, a cure and a preventative are two different things. A cure would ensure healing for all of who are suffering, while a preventative drug will prevent others from suffering altogether. Now, I have no expertise in medicine or pharmaceutical sales, however the idea of managing our time is very similar to medicine. Time management is the pill you need to lower the spread of inefficiencies and the side effects of poor work ethic in your life. You will begin to see long-term success once you maximize your ability to manage time.

Truly mastering the art of Time Management can prevent procrastination, cramming, low-quality work, and even fatigue. When your priorities are not aligned, and you don't value time, the preventatives, in this case, are scheduling, outlining, and goal setting. However, they all begin with prioritizing. Webster dictionary defines the word priority as, "a thing that is regarded as more important than another."

We have a daily investment of 86,400 seconds into your daily life account. Time is valuable, and once you use this daily investment, you cannot get it back. However, if we effectively learn how to manage time, our lives in return will be more productive. Prioritizing allows your actions to align with your purpose. And when your actions and purpose align, you hit peak performance because you understand how your actions, thoughts, and associations impact your ability to fulfill your purpose. When we prioritize, we put the things that are most important at the top of our lists, and we refuse to get sidetracked by anything until we complete the most important tasks. Truth be told, most of our days are filled with completing small, minimal tasks that have very little to do with our overall goal. By the time we are done doing the small things, we have very little energy left to tackle the tasks that matter most. Just because you are doing a lot, doesn't mean you are getting a lot done. Take some time at the beginning of every week to plan and prioritize how you will invest your time. Stop procrastinating and start prioritizing. Stop wasting time and start setting goals.

MAKE THE CHOICE

That one stop light that may have had you stuck for a while was only a speed bump waiting for you to push through to the other side. When you decide you want to do better in your life that is the first stepping out of your circumstance and into your calling.

QUICK ACCOMPLISHMENTS

Demonstrating quick wins are essential to the workplace and build the foundation for long-term morale. Dan Rockwell quoted, "Innovation initiatives require quick wins. But unable to choose is unable to move." In life, when you are winning the small battles, it builds your confidence and slowly prepares you for the war. I was giving a workshop once to a group of high school football players and told them, "it is hard to strive for a perfect season when you are so accustomed to losing." It is hard to meet something that has yet to be measured. Gaining those wins quickly will create a measure of excellence that will allow people to see the value and either want more or decide that it is not for them. Always remember, a bird in the hand is worth two in the bush.

ADAPT

The only thing constant in life is change. The only thing constant in life is change. The only thing constant in life is change. SO, GET USED TO IT! A lot of times with organizational, operational, or general change, you can't automatically expect the people that it is involving to buy into the change. As a leader, the way you approach change is critical to the overall transition into the new way of doing things. You need to adapt your style to speak in a way that resonates with the recipient so they can understand, accept, digest, and adapt. Being an effective leader that inspires change has nothing to do with your circumstance, schooling, or where you are starting. Being a leader who inspires change in the workplace is not a special gift you are born with, it is a skill like any that you can learn. Change starts with an awareness that there is a need to change. It requires courage to explore the unknown and be vulnerable. Inspiring sustainable change requires voluntary buy-in into the change program and a strong leader who will be able to push through the fears.

21 DAYS OF CHANGE

Change is fundamentally essential to growth. The first step to making any change is to commit within yourself. Sometimes, thinking about a change isn't enough. You must go to your bathroom, look yourself in the mirror, and declare that it is time to change. You must let YOU know that you will no longer allow distractions, people, friends, or family take you away from the change that you are trying to make in your life.

At the beginning of one summer, I invited a group of friends to go on 21-day journey of change and transformation with me. During those 21 days, I experienced the true power change can have in one's life. There was a time in my life when I didn't know who I was. I was distracted by people and influenced by circumstance. Quite often, I off track at crucial times, made bad decisions, and invited negativity into my close circles. A good friend of mine always said, "Wherever there is no change is an absence of growth." Everyone talks about changing their appearance to being more beautiful, changing their wardrobe to be trendier, or even changing their residence to fit in with a certain economic status. However, the most beautiful and powerful changes are a change in mindset, attitude, and perspective. When you change these things for the good, you improve who you are as a person. A true interaction with positive change can change the trajectory of your life for the rest of your life.

Instead of joining the majority of people who complain about the condition of the world, join the minority who actually change the world. How do they manage to problem solve and critically think of world-transforming solutions? By first becoming the change that they wish to see in the world. While there are individuals who sit and complain all day, there are actually people out there who work day and night to solve the problems that the majority whine about. You too can become a part of that number. Studies show that it takes 21 days to change any habit – good or bad. Decide today to change your life for the better. Pinpoint habits that you would like to change and commit to 21 days of turning your life around. My 21-day journey did wonders for my confidence, performance, and overall wellbeing. I hope that your 21-day challenge will do the same for you!

For this challenge and the following challenges, you'll need a notebook or your journal.

Part One: Build Your Purpose Plan

Answer the following questions. Be sure to leave space between each goal for part 2!

a. What do you want?
b. Where do you want to go?
c. Who do you want to become?

Part Two: Get Specific

Next to each goal, add the following information.

d. What is your timeline for completing each goal?
e. What is stopping you from getting there?
f. Who/what can help you get there?

TIPS FOR SUCCESS

Take responsibility for your life. Prioritize and do the most important things first.

Define your mission and goals in life. Have an, "Everyone can win!" attitude

Listen to people sincerely. People have important things they could share with you, but you won't learn if you don't listen!

"We as people have to learn how to be uniquely and distinctly great."

– Dr. Ivory Toldson,
Exec. Director of White House Initiatives

CHAPTER TWO

BECOME THE CEO OF YOU

From the day I enrolled in college, I aspired to be a high-powered CEO of a major company. The lifestyle, power, and money intrigued me – especially the money. Many of the things on my long bucket list required money and lots of it. I watched The Wolf of Wall Street, starring Leonardo DiCaprio as the main character, Jordan Belfort. As I watched Belfort fly on private jets, ride on mega yachts, and enjoy the respect and admiration of strangers who dreamed of working for his company, I became enamored with the advantages of his lifestyle. I envied his title and what came with it, but I never understood the responsibility and cost that followed. I was oblivious to obligations like, making all the decisions, dealing with the stress of an unbalanced lifestyle, being accountable for company losses, and having a schedule filled with meetings. Being blinded by the perks of the job, I was completely ignorant of the responsibilities necessary to be successful in the role of a CEO.

THE MISSION PLAN: THE DECISION

I had the opportunity to meet with Steven Hill, the CEO of Aegis Technologies, a privately held small business headquartered in Huntsville, Alabama that specializes in modeling and simulation technology and emerging training solutions for both military and commercial applications. At the time, I was a student at Alabama A&M University in Huntsville, AL and grateful to be in the same room as Mr. Hill. Weeks before the meeting, I prepared the questions I planned to ask, how I would market myself, and a list of reasons why my potential dreams and aspirations could bring value to Aegis and his staff.

At the end of our meeting, I desired to have a job offer or an apprenticeship to learn under the head of the company. However, during that meeting, my whole perspective and aspiration of one day becoming the CEO of my own company changed. Having the opportunity to meet with him at the age of 20 was such a privilege, and the lesson he taught me is one I value to this day. As planned, during our meeting, I explained who I was professionally, my dreams and aspiration, my internship opportunities, the value I could bring to his company, and even presented potential solutions to the problems the company was experiencing at the time.

As I rambled, he sat silently with great professional posture. He wore a nice suit, no tie, and had his black portfolio lying on the desk in front of him. During my entire spill, he listened respectfully, engaged by looking me directly in my eyes and nodding to acknowledge what I said. Now and then, I noticed he would jot something on his tablet. When I saw that one of his notes ended with a question mark, I knew it was time to bring my long-winded speech to a close, catch my breath, and allow Mr. Hill the opportunity to respond. Once I paused, he looked at me, smiled and said, "Son, you have a great vision for your career, but what is the vision for yourself? I know a lot about what you have done, and what you have accomplished; it is astonishing and impressive. I know the professional, but I haven't heard anything of the person. Who is Kyle King?"

At the time, I did not know how to respond, so I looked back at him with confusion. I hadn't studied or prepared to answer that question. Mr. Hill went on to paraphrase some of the things I had mentioned about my dreams of becoming a CEO for a fortune 500 company. I shook my head in agreement. He then asked me the question that he had written on his notepad, "Are you the CEO of yourself?" When he realized that I was taken back and fully unaware of how to answer the question, he took the floor and began to articulate who he was as a person and how everything he does is transferable to his company.

He stated that he ran his business as he ran his household with the same accountability he has a father and husband. He explained how the company's values of integrity, people, and paying it forward are also values that he teaches his children. For Mr. Hill, it wasn't about creating a business plan; the goal was to create a belief system amongst his staff that they can stand behind. "The passion they have for what they do will transfer into creating quality services. It starts within you, not within the title that you hold," Mr. Hill shared.

After our meeting, I still aspired to be a fortune 500 executive, however, I had finally pinpointed the company I wanted to manage – myself. Since then, at the beginning of each

THE MISSION PLAN: THE DECISION

year, I ask myself, "Kyle, are you the CEO of yourself? Where can you make monthly, quarterly, or even yearly adjustments so you can be a high performing company that contributes to the world around you?" Before we dive into the steps of creating the best form of you, I want you to pause and answer the following questions.

Are you the CEO of you?
How is YOUR company performing compared to the competition?
What are your daily, weekly, monthly, quarterly goals to reach your annual targets?

If you are unsure, or answered no to any of the questions above, let's get to work. How do you expect to manage a company, run an organization, coach a team, or even call yourself a leader if you cannot manage your home or your personal finances? If you cannot handle conflict between you and your friends, how do you expect to handle competition in the marketplace? If you are willing to put your life at risk, don't you think that will translate into taking financial or economic risks within your company that could potentially cost you a business deal or the company? You must understand the importance of adopting the position of becoming the CEO of You, Inc. before you can manage the business of the world.

In history, we have seen the effects around the world from years of risk mismanagement. In 2008, specifically, mismanagements led to a worldwide financial crisis that left people homeless and jobless, and sparked an economic depression. Even back in November 2007, before the crisis had really hit the stock markets, one commentator in Financial Times wrote, "It's obvious there has been a massive failure of risk management across most of Wall Street." Life isn't problem proof, and risk happens in business, but understanding how to identify and communicate the risks is critical in rebounding. Understanding how to identify problems and communicate through them doesn't start in the boardrooms but in bedrooms and living rooms. Yes, these skills start right at home. Studies show that the success of CEOs in America is directly linked to how their daily lives operate at home. According to JT Ripton in an article titled, "6 Daily Habits of the World's Most Successful CEOs," there are six habits of many of the world's most successful CEOs.

1. They get up early. Rising early is a nearly universal trait among successful C.E.Os.
2. They exercise regularly.
3. They meditate every day.
4. They cut back on meetings.
5. They organize the details.
6. They cultivate creativity.

In a world where we thrive off international business through multinational enterprises, international organizations, and consultancy companies, rising early through the ranks and joining this business world won't happen by staying in bed until eight or nine in the morning. Kevin Hart, American actor, comedian, writer, and producer told reporters that he starts his day every morning at 5:30 AM with an intense workout. This gives him enough time after his workout to check on his many business ventures, assess goals, and progress moving forward into his day, weeks, and months to come. Kevin Hart is the first comedian ever to make more than Jerry Seinfeld and has changed the economy of the funny business by touring like a rock star. In the Men's Fitness edition featuring Kevin Hart, titled "Kevin Hart is Working Out Harder Than Ever," James Maio writes that Hart is all about "no excuses, no days off." He won't miss a training day, regardless of how much his line of work interferes with his routine, he says. Why? Living a healthy lifestyle makes you better – plain and simple.

How many times in your life do you try to set that alarm to get up early and go on a run, pray, or even study for that test and you are still tired from the night before? How many times do you hit the snooze button? How many different alarms does it take you to get out of bed? How many times have you done that same method and ended up not studying for that major exam, being late for the Monday meeting at work, or even skipping that early morning workout because you just didn't have enough time? Getting up early will give you the extra time to make it easier for you to incorporate those innovative ideas into You, Inc. Regardless your age, exercising regularly is almost the most common attribute among successful CEOs; getting up early sets this foundation.

During track season in college, we had 6:30 AM team workouts. We would jog for five miles followed by a light lift and an active stretching series. I hated every minute of waking up, but then I began to realize that the hardest part was getting out of the bed. I began to use the morning workouts as reflection time to prepare for the day ahead and a spark to start my day on the right foot. I used the workout to de-stress from the day before, the past failures, or even the future problems to arise in the future. I used this time to form my thoughts, strategize for the long day ahead.

Even though I'm no longer in college or on a track team, I still use running and writing as my form of meditation to clear my mind and focus on the goals and the dreams ahead. During one of Oprah Winfrey's many televised interviews, she talked about her devotion to the practice of transcendental meditation (TM). She even hired TM instructors for her company so that her employees could learn the art and practice of meditation. Until I watched that interview, I never believed in meditation. I always told my friends that my work was my form of peace and that if you are doing what you love to do, you won't ever have to get away. I believed that one's success should be tranquility. When I hesitantly put prayer and meditation into my daily schedule, I began to truly understand and feel the effects of real peace, tranquility, and calmness of mind. The quality of my work, relationships, and happiness improved tremendously.

Meditation allowed me to take all that I had on my plate and organize it so my life could run more smoothly. I positioned myself to make an impactful difference in my life and the contributions I made to the world. Part of being the CEO of You is not just focusing on being the "Chief" Executive; but also the creative executor. You must understand how to cultivate creativity. Creativity or innovation is the bloodline of any business. It inspires not only the art of success but the sustainability of success. As the creator, visionary, and innovator, if you learn how to master these habits, whether it be in your living room at home or the boardroom at your office, you will set the foundation for making a major impact in your

THE MISSION PLAN: THE DECISION

life and the world around you.

First things first: Remember that the home is where the foundation is built to be effective in the workplace. Before anyone can adopt a code of conduct for their Fortune 500 company, they must first adopt a code of conduct for themselves. When we look at different companies and organizations around the world, there is always a mention about their various and unique company cultures. An organization's culture encompasses the general attitudes, norms, and values that define the company. A positive culture aids in retaining current employees and attracting the top talent for new opportunities and job openings. Routines play a key role in establishing the acceptable norms and behaviors within the workplace. How well are you managing yourself, family, and household? Take a moment to answer the following questions.

What culture do you have within your household with your family?

What are the general attitude, norms, and values that define your family name?

Will that be passed down to your children and spread amongst those closest to you?

Do you have a positive culture and a sense of comradery in your household where your children or even your spouse feel comfortable enough to speak to you about problems or potential solutions?

What daily routines have you established to keep you focused and accountable for accomplishing your daily, weekly and monthly goals?

YOUR SUCCESS STARTS AT SUN RISE

Researchers have written that the first hour of your day sets the tone for the rest of the day. What you do, what you think about and what you choose to put your attention on determines how much you will accomplish for the rest of your day. It is important as winners, that we become aware of how we are spending that first hour so we can perform at our highest level of efficiency. Successful entrepreneurs and business professionals have figured out the formula that the first hour of your day can dictate the productivity level for the rest of the day. It is important that before the chaos consumes your brain to use this crucial bucket of time to ensure you are leading a day focused on results, not on reactions.

My First Hour

5:00 AM – Wake up to the song, Early Riser by Taylor McFerrin
5:15 AM – Write in my Gratitude Journal (How am I feeling? What am I feeling? What am I grateful for?)
5:30 AM – Pray, read daily devotional & meditate (Read scripture and have ten minutes of complete silence)
6:00 AM – Review my day (Check schedule & prepare for meetings)

Five Questions I Ask Myself

1. What is today going to look like?
2. What do you hope to accomplish today?
3. Where are you going to win today?
4. What do you fear today?
5. How are you going to overcome that fear?

THE MISSION PLAN: THE DECISION

Every morning I choose to focus on three things that keep me focused throughout my day: Having a day that is productive, remaining positive, and having all of my tasks align with my purpose. By setting the foundation within the first hour, it helps me to remain happy, stress-free and performing at a high level of excellence.

BE PRODUCTIVE

The majority of people are busy with tasks, deadlines, and even assignments but not many people have mastered being productive with the results in mind. Productivity isn't something you just fall into, it is a practice, an art, and a focused effort on flawlessly executing no matter the circumstances. People that are busy usually fill their time with meaningless tasks without focusing on the result; while people that are productive use less time and get more done with maximizing the results in mind. Prioritizing this first hour in your day is the foundation to the productivity level throughout the rest of your day.

Questions to Ask
What do I want to accomplish today?
What are my goals for today?
What do I need to cut out today?

BE POSITIVE

Every single morning before I shower, before I get my son dressed for school, and even before I walk out of the door; I look in the mirror and say three positive affirmations about myself. You have to believe in yourself before anyone will believe in you. Positive thinking starts with you! I read once that "self-talk is the endless stream of unspoken thoughts that run through your head, whether negative or positive". If the thoughts that run through your head are mostly negative, your outlook on life is mostly negative. If your thoughts are filled with positivity, you're likely an optimist that focuses on the possibilities and not the problems. Your thoughts have a direct impact on the outcome of your day, your goals, and your dreams. Articulating positive affirmations daily, provides the opportunity for you to hear true and empowering statements that first humble you and revert you back to your core values.

Say This Daily
I am worthy!
I am beautiful!
I am courageous!
I am excited about today!
Today is going to be a great day!
I am one step closer!
I am blessed!

BE PURPOSEFUL

Don't get so caught up in being a professional, where you lose sight of your life's purpose. My parents used to always tell me, "don't be so busy trying to make a living, where you forget to live your life." The true nature of life is not to just be happy or fulfilled, it is to be valuable, useful and compassionate while making a difference in other people's lives. Every day I take time and sit and focus on what I am here for, how am I going to be useful and how am I going to contribute to making someone's day better. This is the moment where I am not thinking with my head, but with my heart because your heart is your best tool to access your true passion and life's purpose. It is important for you to not live a life of existence, but to live a life of meaning.

Questions to Ask
How am I going to make a difference?
Who am I going to help today?
How am I going to be useful today?

When I graduated college, I fell into the trap of having too much time before and after work. I wasted more time, effort, and resources than I utilized. I started to gain weight and lose track of time. Time began to own me. One day, I looked in the mirror and realized that I was 20 pounds heavier, with dark circles under my eyes from a lack of sleep. It wasn't that I didn't have time to sleep, in fact, most nights I got in bed at a decent time. Once in bed, I couldn't sleep from tossing and turning with thoughts about my discomfort with my life. Truth be told, I wasn't happy with the road I was headed down. Immediately after my discovery of my condition, I created a daily schedule that I still use now.

Leadership in our lives is not something we are born into; it is something learned, mastered, and developed. It first starts with taking the time to self-reflect, being honest with yourself, identifying areas of improvement, and analyzing your strengths and weaknesses so you can act in this new developmental process.

During a Podcast by Simon Sinek, author of Start with Why and Leaders Eat Last, he described this concept of leadership being a developed trait that can be compared to working out in the gym or even building a relationship with someone. As a former college athlete, I completely understood what he meant by the whole idea of working out. Our coaches would always preach consistency and tell us to trust the process. We wouldn't see results overnight. True progress is a process that takes slow steps of growth. Further in the podcast, he broke down the comparison by explaining the process to getting into shape. We cannot just go to the gym one day for nine hours and expect to see great results in the mirror the next day; it is a gradual process. If we go back to the gym every day to work out for 30 minutes, eventually, we will begin to see results. We will feel the changes, lightness, and extra boost of energy. We may even become more motivated to live a healthier lifestyle. Our bodies will begin to crave more fruits and vegetables, and we will begin to get enough sleep because of the late-night runs on the treadmill or at the track. Just by making those few changes in our lifestyles, we will have a heightened sense of happiness and peace that will contribute to us living a longer and more prosperous life.

It is very similar to dating. We don't go on one date, immediately fall in love, and no longer feel a need to date that person – at least we shouldn't. Dating is a process. A process of communicating, getting to know one another, and showing compassion and consistent love for each other. One day, you begin to look at each other differently, feel differently, and start to say, "I love you." Does that make sense? Well, this same concept applies to life. We cannot work hard on Monday and Tuesday and expect to see results by Wednesday. To see the results we desire to see in our lives, we must consistently work productive routines day in and day out, sometimes stretching on for weeks, months, and maybe even years. Eventually, the routine will become a part of you and cause you to think and act differently. One day, you will wake up and notice a number in your bank account that you once only dreamed of seeing. Arthur Ashe, one of the greatest professional tennis players, quoted, "Success is a journey, not a destination. The doing is often more important than the outcome." Ashe always spoke about his intense process of greatness in sports and his commitment to social justice, health, and humanitarian issues. By using and sharing wisdom like this, he left a mark on the world as incredible as his mark on sports.

During the early stages of my career, I had an opportunity to speak at the Keystone Success Conference for the Boys and Girls Club of Northern Alabama. The purpose of the conference is to provide Keystones with positive opportunities to engage and socialize with peers, explore teen issues relevant to their lives, and develop skills to support and enhance service and leadership efforts in their various Clubs and communities. That year, the theme for the conference was, "The year of YOU." When presented this opportunity, I was elated and looked forward to being on the stage addressing hundreds of boys and girls from the Huntsville community and different surrounding areas.

Three weeks before the address, my excitement began to go down as I prepared the direction I wanted to take when presenting to students. My previous experience with speaking was in more professional settings where I discussed business, innovative ideas, and even success strategies. The Boys and Girls Club was a different crowd, and I didn't want to talk to my audience, I wanted to talk with them. With help from a close friend of mine, we broke the whole speech down into three parts. We understood that our message, brand, and experiences would hit the audience more effectively if we engaged with the students as we taught them the importance of the word YOU and how we must conquer self before we can go out and conquer the world. The speech was simplified into the following acronym:

Y - INVEST in Yourself
O - Seize Opportunities
U - Upgrade Your Knowledge, Involvement, and Circle)

At the time I delivered this speech, there were many times in my life where I wasn't true to myself and allowed others to influence my decisions and what I did. I didn't worry about the milestones that were approaching and only focused on the moment. At some point in our lives, we've all been guilty of allowing the minor things to have a major impact on our lives, dreams, and destiny.

So, with this acronym, I want to challenge you to invest in yourself by:

- understanding who you are
- knowing what your strengths are
- determining what you want
- planning what the rest of your day, week, month and year look like for you.

Once you know what you want, and where you are going, you will be ready to seize opportunities as they present themselves. As you seize opportunities, you will grow in knowledge, and begin to meet and rub shoulders with influential people in your area of expertise. This is how you will upgrade your involvement and circle. You will begin to connect with people who invest in you instead of being surrounded by the expenses of inadequacy.

Have you ever walked into a store in the mall and tried to find an outfit for a big event, party, or gathering and found yourself becoming frustrated with the clutter and disorganization of the racks? Did the number of items out of place or just piled on top of each other caused you to become stressed? Or, have you ever felt this same stress or frustration with your own closet as you sorted through new clothes, old clothes, dirty clothes, clothes you've only worn once, and clothes you no longer fit? Now, ask yourself this same question about your social and interpersonal environment. Take some time and analyze the purpose of the people in your circle and the value they add to your life? If you are like me and millions of other people, it is time to unclutter your interpersonal environment, understand the importance of upgrading your closet of contributors, and see the positive or negative impacts of your circle of friends.

In Jerry Gillis' 1976 book, FRIENDS – The Power and Potential of The Company You Keep, he talks about the importance our supportive interpersonal environments, composed of friends who make you feel good and bring out the best in you. In the book, he quoted, "Make a clean sweep! Get rid of boring friends, whining friends, hostile friends, friends who will talk your ear off, and friends who will sit quietly by, saying and doing nothing, letting you carry the whole burden of the conversation and the relationship. Trim down your list of friends to those who really inspire you, and you'll find you have time and energy." Now, this isn't easy, because many of us, including myself, at times fall into the trap of wanting to be liked by everybody and feeling like you don't want to disappoint anyone. But, I want you to take the time and think about the time and energy you have wasted holding onto friendships that are toxic, relationships that aren't going anywhere, or situations that bring out the worst in you. Out of the acronym YOU above, upgrading is the most critical point and crucial step as you walk into that board room and manage You, Inc. We will discuss upgrading more in-depth in the next chapter. Before we focus on upgrading, I want you to take a moment and focus in on you, your environment, your opportunities, and your circle.

In a book, I recently read titled, The People Factor: How Building Great Relationships and Ending Bad Ones Unlock Your God-Given Purpose Van Moody quotes, "You need to be around people who challenge you to grow and who refuse to allow you to settle for mediocrity."

So, as stated above, I want to challenge you to invest in yourself by understanding who you are and what you must offer to the world. Secondly, begin to seize those opportunities as they present themselves to you. As those opportunities come and you begin to gain experience, this will set the foundation in upgrading your circle of influence and ultimately investing in the longevity of You, Inc.

I said you would need a notebook or your journal! Answer the following questions honestly.

Part One: Y
1. What are my strengths and weaknesses?
2. What am I passionate about?
3. Where am I naturally gifted?

Part Two: O
4. What opportunities have I currently been presented? (friends, connections, jobs, internships, relationships, etc.)

Answer for each opportunity you list.

5. What will I learn from these opportunities?
6. Do these opportunities align with my future goals and dreams?
7. Will these opportunities get me closer to complete happiness and success?

Part Three: U
8. Who is in my close circle?

Answer for each individual you listed.

9. Does this person support my goals?
10. Does this person challenge me to grow and refuse to settle for mediocrity?
11. Does this person add to my happiness and wellbeing?

TIPS FOR SUCCESS

One of the greatest forces on this planet is the power of believing in you.

Your passion, skills, and conviction is all you need to live the best life possible and fulfill your hearts every wish and desire. That one belief can part seas, move mountains, and even create opportunities.

Tune out the negativity and begin to trust in the little voice over the You, Inc. intercom.

"The only limit to our realization of tomorrow will be our doubts of today."

– Franklin D. Roosevelt

CHAPTER THREE
DIVINE RIGHT OR DESTINY

A 2006 drama, The Illusionist, starring Jessica Biel and Edward Norton takes viewers back to the late nineteenth century Vienna telling a tale of the renowned illusionist, Eisenheim, being reunited with the Duchess von Teschen and how love conquers over Crown Prince Leopold's corrupt pursuit of power. During one of Eisenheim's performances, he is challenged by the arrogant and power-hungry Crown Prince Leopold to perform a trick "without all of the gadgetry." Eisenheim agrees and begins his monologue as the cameras catch him walking to the edge of the stage holding Crown Prince Leopold's sword between his hands. Eisenheim begins his soon to be devastating trick with a question, "Where does power flow from? Skill or destiny, or divine right?" He continues his monologue by reminding the audience of the story of the sword, Excalibur. Eisenheim articulates, "Excalibur was fixed in stone and then it stayed. Many knights tried to pull this sword out of the stone which all failed. Only King

Arthur succeeded, proving his right to rule. Who can take this sword?"

Luck, skill, opportunity, environment, and many other words are used to define people's success, but I am here to tell you that you are the King and Queen Arthur of your destiny. It is up to you and only you to pull the sword of success out of the stone of fear. You are the rightful heir to achievement, and your attributes are associated with the rightful sovereignty of your succession. Jacquelyn Smith presents a strong argument in her 2014 article, "This is How Americans Define Success," stating that according to Merriam-Webster, success is "the fact of getting or achieving wealth, respect, or fame." But a new survey from Strayer University suggests that it may be time to update the dictionary's definition. The school recently released findings from its national Success Project Survey, which was conducted to determine what success means to Americans today. A whopping 90% believe that success is more about happiness than power, possessions, or prestige. A nationally recognized entrepreneur, author, women's activist, and great friend of mine, Loreal Jones, would describe it this way, "There is a difference between worldly success and destiny success. Worldly success is being remembered for your possessions, but destiny success is being remembered for everything you are as a person."

With a bachelor's degree in finance and years of experience in my field, I assure you that the best investment I have ever made was the investment in myself. Investing in Corporate America could bring great returns and dividends that could lead to a nice home or even beautiful vacations. However, investing in your destiny success could bring you a fortune capable of creating intergenerational wealth. Lao Tzu, ancient Chinese philosopher, reputed author of the Tao Te Ching and founder of philosophical Taoism, quoted, "If you know when you have enough, you are wealthy, if you carry your intentions to completion, you are resolute, if you live a long and creative life, you will leave an eternal legacy." The term legacy is more profound than any quote, saying, or dictionary definition. Legacy is an ongoing activity, and it is what you do between here and eternity. The legacy of tomorrow is captured by seizing the opportunities of today. Creating a legacy is the pathway that leads to a deeper sense of significance beyond the pursuit of success and following it results in a positive impact of society.

Most people define opportunity as a set of circumstances that make it possible to do something. But I define it as a group of experiences that makes it possible to turn your dream into a reality. Turn your reality into a long-term positively impactful legacy that will be left long after you have graduated from that college, retired from that company, or left this earth. While attending Alabama A&M University, I was invited to many conferences and forums and offered a variety of different opportunities for career and professional development simply because of my connections and circles. In the book we mentioned earlier, The People Factor: How Building Great Relationships and Ending Bad Ones Unlocks Your God-Given Purpose by Van Moody he states, "The quality of our lives and our experiences is determined by the people that we are connected to."

A multitude of opportunities is constantly in front of our faces, passing by us like a line of eighteen-wheelers on the interstate. When we see eighteen-wheelers, or any large mode of transportation for that matter, we move out the way, slow down so they can pass us, or even speed up and pass them by. Instead of being afraid of being run over or off the road, we must identify the benefits of these opportunities and begin to pursue them. These actions of pursuit will force us to take risks, solve problems, and even become uncomfortable. Stepping outside of our comfort zones is necessary.

In college, I was afforded many opportunities to intern with companies and organizations like NASA, The United States Department of Agriculture, BMW, Tennessee Valley Authority, and Volvo Cars of North America. I even spent a summer in Ghana as a geopolitical intern. Each of these opportunities was given to me by people I'd connected with, shared my vision with, or made intentions to introduce myself to. None of my opportunities would have been possible if I stayed secluded from the world and refused to connect with the opportunities around me. Being in the right place at the right time can shift your life and make your future dreams your current realities.

In my early twenties, at the beginning of my career, I had the opportunity to be among some very influential, ambitious, and hardworking individuals in Huntsville, AL. I contributed to the organization of a very successful event at an airplane Hangar for NOVA, Inc. NOVA's mission, at the time, was to bring together young professionals 21 to 35 years old and use the gathering as a platform to connect people and integrate business and social networks. Once a week, we met at a specified location to plan a major event that the city had never witnessed. The plan was to revolutionize the Huntsville scene and create a paradigm shift for years to come. Every week, young professionals from different backgrounds, ethnicities, genders, industries, and social statuses came together and used each other's knowledge and experience to coordinate this dream event to benefit one of the local charities in town. We were a group of people that had never met, were not getting paid, and had absolutely no tangible incentives for running the project, however, we exhibited real teamwork and got things done. Our only reason for participating was a desire to be a part of a plan that could help the Huntsville Community. It wasn't about the opportunity to have a successful event; it was about the opportunity to have our hands in something that would positively impact the community. It was about the chance to work on a team, serve its importance, and the output of quality, morale, and retention.

Each week, we shared ideas such as potential sponsors, marketing techniques, funding opportunities, vendors, the specific community groups that would be present, etc. The leadership team delegated tasks to the core team, and we worked collectively to get things done. I had some of the best times of my life because we enjoyed such a sense of comradery and mutual buy-in. This was also the most unorthodox and unstructured team that I have ever been a part of. There was no exact direction, and there were many potential contingencies that could have ruined the event. However, that beautiful night of May 21, 2016, Nova threw a successful Hangar Party with enough sponsorships to cover all their expenses. Over 1,200 people attended the event, more than 70 community organizations were present, and everyone in attendance had an excellent time. Throughout the evening,

I mingled with the guests and introduced myself to as many people as possible and at the end of the night, pocketed about 50-60 business cards that have already served as business contacts and continue to open doors for me to this day.

In life, we will experience opportunities and things that will serve as a spark or catalyst to our success. We can't allow these life-changing experiences to pass us by; we must embrace them. These are the experiences and opportunities that will help us progress. I believe that the experience I gained working with NOVA Inc. shifted my life and was a key contributor to my current success. Sometimes, the bottom-line isn't about the bottom line, and we must participate in serving our communities. Community service has transformed me into a more open-minded and compassionate person with a bigger heart and a willingness to sacrifice for others.

Being in the right place at the right time with the right motives could truly change your life and taking advantage of opportunities could take you from being a random person with dreams to a respected force in your field.

As you begin to set goals and build your personal and professional network, connect with people who can open doors for you. This process is all part of the upgrading we discussed in Chapter Two. You must transition from a young woman or man with a desire to a person who lives within their destiny. You must approach every day as an opportunity to align your actions with your purpose and align your commitments to your calling.

After you understand that YOU are the captain of your ship and you hold the keys to your destiny, you must have a plan of action for moving forward. Inefficiencies in the form of bad habits, such as wasting time, procrastinating, and making uninformed or bad decisions take away from your brand and over time can decrease your overall net worth. In business, your biggest asset is the ability to earn income, and you cannot earn income if your business has a bad reputation. Therefore, knowing your weaknesses and having a plan of action to deal with them is crucial. In life, one of our biggest assets is the ability to acquire knowledge and upgrade our education, involvement, and circle.

UPGRADE YOUR EDUCATION

Upgrading your education is key to upgrading your personal hard drive. In one of his many profound speeches, Malcolm X quoted, "Education is the passport to the future, for tomorrow belongs to those who prepare for it today." Education is a basic human right and a significant factor in the development of children, communities, and countries. Education can help contribute to the fight against HIV/AIDS, reducing hunger, improving child survival and maternal health, empowering women and girls, and even building peace amongst nations. Many students and educators of this generation do not understand that education goes further than what is being taught in the classroom. Being able to integrate real-life application with theoretical knowledge is where true education and hands-on knowledge come together. Julian Hall once quoted, "Knowledge is useless without consistent application." There have been many changes in the Educational System in America. While revolutions in technology have made information so much more accessible, this has hurt the process of critically thinking.

THE MISSION PLAN: THE DECISION

Ignorance and the miseducation of the public, in general, has led to global epidemics of violence, anger, and hatred among different races and ethnicities. Andrew Smith, author of Lost in a Pyramid, once quoted, "People fear what they don't understand and hate what they can't conquer." Through life and experience, I've found the truth in Smith's quote. When people do not feel comfortable asking the difficult questions to learn about others different from themselves, they live in fear.

Upgrading is a fundamental shift in your life that requires you to align every action with your purpose. With computer hardware, an upgrade is very important for ultimate performance and efficiency. Adding new hardware to a computer improves its performance. With upgraded hardware, you can get a huge boost in performance, and an upgrade to the RAM will contribute to the computer running more smoothly.

I have fallen into the 20th-century trap of upgrading my iPhone every year or every chance a new iPhone releases, compared to some of my friends who have had their same phones for years at a time. Sometimes, upgrading depends on what punctualities you are looking for or, in terms of technology, what features you want or need to see a huge boost in performance. You must learn how to think critically, become an expert in your field, and learn something new every day about either yourself, your industry, your team, your spouse, or just life in general. Knowledge begins at the end of a sentence and the beginning of a question mark. Thomas Berger quoted, "The art and science of asking questions is the source of all knowledge."

In school, many of us have been shunned for asking questions. Personally, I was looked upon as uneducated and far from intelligent. Experiences like these often cause our view of learning to become skewed. Many of those same feelings transfer over into the workplace when we are placed in a learning environment. The fear of learning new things can translate into ultimately disliking new policies, new people or protocols and maybe even better ways of doing things. I believe that education is the universal tool to truly becoming a better citizen, businessman or woman, and overall person. The better understanding we have of any subject, the more insight we have on problem-solving for our future. Being informed about your business makes you more effective in every way, whether it is closing a business deal or communicating with your partner. If you are a student, upgrade those study habits and the amount of time and focus you put towards your educational experience. If you are looking for direction or are unsure of what field to focus on in work, then take some time learning about different industries and jobs. Look up trends in a variety of markets and see what direction the world is trending in the future. If you are in business, learn what your business did well, what it did wrong, and how you can capitalize on your competitor's weaknesses while saving money to bring in higher revenue next quarter. Every day you wake up is an opportunity to learn something, so take a class, read a book, gain knowledge of some kind that you didn't have the day before. Take advantage of every opportunity to learn.

UPGRADE YOUR INVOLVEMENT

As we discussed, learning the true value of education goes much further than sitting in a classroom or a lecture hall and preparing for a test. Each experience and interaction is an opportunity to gain a better understanding of who you are and the direction in which you are headed. Benjamin Franklin said, "Tell me and I forget. Teach me and I remember. Involve me and I learn." Education is more than memorization for a quiz, exam, or presentation; it is the application and inclusion of knowledge that challenges our mind. Education is the point where what you learn meets what you do. One way to educate yourself is to upgrade your overall involvement in the community.

Volunteer or work with someone you can even learn from. Every experience you have builds on what you already know. Being involved is one way to learn outside of the classroom and boardroom. You gain a chance to put yourself into problem-solving solutions and increase your ability to be solution-minded instead of problem-filled. Each opportunity that you take to get involved is an opportunity to bring something more to the table when you are interacting, interviewing or maybe even inspiring others.

The people and activities you are involved with should be positive influences on you and add value to your life, not take anything away. There is true power in surrounding yourself with positive influences. Bill Davis quoted, "Positive thoughts generate positive feelings and attractive positive people to attach positive life experiences." I truly believe that the most significant rewards in life are the personal sacrifices we make on behalf of others to help them grow and reach their full potential. A strong relationship starts with two people who are ready to sacrifice every and anything for each other. From there, you begin to build a foundation based upon service and not leadership. The best leadership or leaders in our society are the ones who understood the true importance of service.

As a child, I was always taught to give back. Whether it was helping incoming students get to class, leading voters to the registration counter to exercise their right to vote, or developing tutoring programs for underrepresented schools in Huntsville City, I did what I could. Muhammad Ali quoted, "Service to others is the rent you pay for your room here on earth." My personal commitment to service never stopped on the campus of Alabama A&M University, or in the Huntsville community and I don't believe yours should ever stop either.

Community service generates a feeling and teaches a life lesson similar to many concepts learned only through hands-on experience. There is something so fulfilling and unique that comes with giving back to one's community. Maybe it's the satisfaction of helping those who may not otherwise receive help. Perhaps it is the gained sensitivity of the needs of others or a life made more meaningful. My involvement in the community has made me not only a better man but also a better businessman and has helped me to come to understand the community. I remember hearing a George Foreman quote, "Filling a need is not merely good business; it is a basic attitude towards life. If you see a need, do whatever you can do to meet that need." Knowing the community has helped me to provide products and services to meet their basic needs. My involvement in the community has connected me with various donors, philanthropists, and people interested in supporting my philanthropic or profitable endeavors. But most importantly, my involvement in the community has contributed to the growth in not only the community but those who live within it as well. My Alma Mater's famous motto is, "Service is Sovereignty." I still live by that to this day. Regardless of how successful I become professionally or financially, the opportunity to put a hand back and pull the next generation up is, in my opinion, the ultimate form of true leadership. As Clarence Clemons quotes, "Being involved in the well-being and advancement of one's own community is a most natural thing to do."

UPGRADE YOUR CIRCLE

Jeff Boss, executive coach, entrepreneur, speaker, former Navy SEAL, and author of Navigating Chaos and Managing the Mental Game: How to Think More Effectively, Navigate Uncertainty and Build Mental Fortitude wrote, "The ability to influence others through words or behavior is an incredibly valuable tool in your relationship toolbox." In a recent article published in the Entrepreneur Magazine, "4 Surefire Ways to Grow Your Circle of Influence," he presented four strategies to learn how to expand your circle of entrepreneurial influence. As we close this chapter, we will discuss each.

1. Do what you say
2. Choose your battles
3. Be present
4. Grow yourself

Do what you say.

I heard a saying once that "Words are meaningless without intent and follow through." To this day, it has stuck with me because it is so true. Words mean absolutely nothing if you do not follow through with your actions. While you are upgrading your circle, this is very important because you want to be a person of your word even if you must go out of your way to do so. If you say you are going to do something, the words you speak should be bonded with action. By being a person of your word, you increase your credibility and make yourself available for more opportunities. You become not a person of success but a person of moral value. By always having integrity, being trustworthy, and reliable, you will be well respected amongst your peers or colleagues. As Les Brown quotes, "Honor your commitments with integrity."

Choose your battles.

When you start looking at situations as a "win" instead of a battle where there is only one winner, your life will shift. We must be careful how we frame situations in our mind because the words we use to define them, whether they are just thoughts or impactful words, have a great deal of power for the tone of communication we ensue. When we look at conversations as a "battle," we assume an adversarial position and put up our guards. We become defensive instead of understanding, and we make assumptions based upon opinion instead of arguments based upon facts. As you upgrade your circle, focus on the content of the message, not exposing someone's flaws or weaknesses. Give people your full attention and focus on the nature of the conversation. Be understanding so you can come out with the best solution for both parties – not just what works best for you at that given moment. This will build a form of trust and understanding among all involved and will create an empathic connection that promotes even greater openness. The next time you think you are getting into a heated conversation or a debate, listen instead of being on the defense. It is okay to agree to disagree, but not at the expense of degrading another person's character or viewpoints. Remember, when we are faced with tough situations, the way we engage during the process will determine the outcome.

Be present.

During my travels, I sat next to a woman with whom I later developed a great friendship. We connected through a mutual interest in the book I was reading at the time, Essentialism: The Disciplined Pursuit of Less by Greg McKeown. I mentioned to her that it was one of the most enlightening and impactful books I have read and explained how it had made a positive shift in my life. After reading Essentialism, I began new habits and saw life through a different lens gathering a new perspective. Our conversation was so intriguing that I forgot that I was on a plane had been delayed four hours, had an AC that didn't work, and was experiencing so much turbulence that the flight attendants couldn't serve beverages. As we chatted, she mentioned how she had learned to not think about the past or worry about the future, but to be present at the moment. "When you are not living in the moment, you miss out on the previous experiences and memories," she explained. If you are going to live a fulfilled life, you must fully grasp the message of that statement. When we focus on past success, past failure, future opportunities, or potential problems, we miss out on the moments that are happening right in front of us. We are miss out on the lessons and experiences we should be grateful for. As you upgrade your circle, enjoy the moment and understand how to live in the present. This will allow you to build healthier, more beneficial, and more impactful relationships in every area of your life. Enjoy the time that you share with others. Don't be so focused on the future dream that you miss the beauty of the current reality.

Grow yourself.

We don't grow when things are easy; we grow when we face challenges. The purpose is to understand this skill and the importance of maturing. Grow to love yourself because you are ultimately the person you spend every waking minute with. Spend time getting to know who you are so you can understand the type of people that would best fit your circle. It is mutually beneficial for both you and the people in your circle. As you add value to others, you will increase your value. Bloom where you are planted and nurture your fruits daily; whether that be picking up a new book, listening to a podcast, or learning a new recipe to cook for dinner. The most difficult thing in life is understanding and getting to know yourself, but the more you know, the more you will grow.

Pull out your notebook or journal and answer the following questions.

Part One: Education

1.   Do you know enough information about the things you are interested in?
2.   How can you acquire more information?
3.   What classes or certifications are available to you?
4.   What internships or shadow opportunities are available to you?

Part Two: Involvement

5.   Are there opportunities to serve within your community, school, or church?
6.   If not, what are some ways that you create opportunities to serve?
7.   If so, what opportunities are available?
8.   Why haven't you taken advantage of opportunities to serve?
9.   What changes will you make to increase your involvement?

Part Three: Your Circle

10. What changes can you make to begin upgrading your circle today?

11. What interest groups or clubs would you like to be a part of and why?

12. How will your involvement with these groups increase your ability to pursue your purpose?

13. What steps will you take to begin connecting with these groups?

TIPS FOR SUCCESS

Don't listen to others, define what success means to you. Then, and only then will you be able to accurately measure how close you are to achieving success. Additionally, your definition of success will help you align your goals to what it is you want to achieve.

Review your life. If there is any negativity, do everything within your power to remove it. If you can't remove it, set your mind on how you will process it moving forward.

Everything you do, say, or participate in determines your legacy. Before you make any decisions, big or small, ask yourself, "How will this impact my legacy?"

"Success is most often achieved by those who don't know that failure is inevitable."

- Coco Chanel

CHAPTER FOUR
OBSERVE, LEARN, & GROW

One of my good friends always says, "Everybody cannot be in the front row of your life. You have to build quality relationships with qualified people." Remember, you are the director of the movie that you are producing and everyone shouldn't be a part of making the movie. At the end of every movie is a long list of credits. Those credits include people, companies, and resources used to create the film. Whether the film tops the box office and breaks records, or the film flops and doesn't meet its expected projections, those people in the credits were still a part of the production and will still be recognized at the end of the film.

In life, you have to look at your life as the motion picture, you are the director, and all the people around you are a part of the credits at the end of your movie. Everyone doesn't deserve to be a part of that list for this successful record-breaking film you are producing. You have to have applications, selections, and hiring processes to see if people are qualified

THE MISSION PLAN: THE DECISION

to be involved in what you are trying to produce and manifest in your life. One bad apple spoils the bunch, and you do not want too many apples that will negatively impact the rest of your life. In a world of commerce focused on quantity, supply, and demand, there is a low demand for quality and a high demand for innovation. Steve Jobs quoted, "Be a yard stick of quality. Some people aren't used to an environment where excellence is expected." Instead of settling for that friend who you've known your whole life, that girlfriend or boyfriend who just makes you feel comfortable, or the supporter who is there at times and gone the next, create a standard of excellence and you will begin to attract what you set. What you do, is what you attract, and you can either step forward into growth or step back into safety. The first step toward growth is a positive change, and the first step toward failure is a bad habit. As you commit to your calling, you will invite more critics to be able to add their thoughts, opinions, and third-party comments.

However, upgrading your circle is understanding the importance of not taking criticism from those who have not constructed anything at all. Kenneth Tynan said it best when he quoted, "A critic, is a man who knows the way, but can't drive the car."

I do not understand how people who need to borrow money for rent every month feel like the best financial advisors. Or, how people who have never been married, are single, or are always in and out of relationships have positioned themselves as love/relationship coaches. I'm sure you know a few people who fit into these categories and others that are similar. Be cautious of receiving the instruction they have deemed suitable for your situation. Do not let questionable critics bankrupt you of valuable energy that could be better utilized working on your discipline. Take the time to consider in advance how you will handle your critics to keep your critics from handling you and influencing your decisions. Stop allowing critics to drive your decisions, life, and dreams and take back the wheel of opportunity and success.

KEEP YOUR HEAD IN THE GAME

During games when I played sports in high school and college, my coaches would advise the team to zone out the crowd and not worry about anything but what is happening on the court – especially during crunch time. It was difficult to zone out screaming and cheering fans, people dressed up as mascots, and big signs, however, learning this habit came in handy for me in the long run. I have heard stories of professional athletes who have songs in their heads during the loudest and most pressure-filled times of the game. It amazes me when musicians perform in crowds of thousands and still deliver a great performance. I never understood how they did it without getting nervous. The truth is, it is hard to "just block out" the crowd and all the noise. It is hard when the world, the game, and life is just a loud place. It is hard when there are four seconds on the clock in the fourth quarter, you have the ball, everyone wants you to shoot a three to win the game, but you want to lay it up to just tie it. It is hard to concentrate when so many people are yelling and saying so many different things, it's hard to concentrate and make the best decision for the desired outcome. I implore you to consider these questions: At any sporting event, who is the loudest person during the game? The coach? The player? Or, the onlookers? Now, I want you to ask yourself this: During your trials, tribulations, mistakes, and failures, who usually is the loudest person in your life? Is it your mentors, coaches, or supporters? Or, is it the haters, friends, or critics? The lesson here is for you to learn how to silence the crowd. Don't think about the words or loud advice. Follow the silent prompting in your mind. Think about what you're going to do when you get the ball and what plays you should make to create a good opportunity for your teammates. Keep your head in the game and not in the stands. Focus on what is happening in the game instead of what is going on around the game. The crowd can and often will be loud, annoying, frustrating, obnoxious, and even angry, but you must keep your eyes and mind on the game and stay focused on the mission at hand. You are the star player in this game we call life. Do not let the instructions from the stands, or the screams from the courtside, or the distractions of your surrounding detour your focus. The loudest person is always in the stands, WATCHING, and the best players are on the court PLAYING. The more success you gain, the higher you go up. The better you do, the more people are going to scream, but you want people in your circle screaming positivity and motivation, and pushing you to go further in life.

KNOW YOUR PRODUCT

When I was 23 years old, I transitioned from Alabama to start working with Janssen Biotechnology, Inc., a subsidiary company of Johnson & Johnson, Inc., to be a pharmaceuticals sales representative. Even though pharmaceutical sales are known as being the "Golden Handcuffs" of jobs because of all the perks, financial bonuses, and opportunities to travel, network, and make your work schedule, I still had my eye set on my purpose – not on profit. At the time, I had serious plans of working my way back to Huntsville, where my non-profit organization was located. I was interested in being a leader in the paradigm shift that was taking place.

Before leaving, I looked at several residences and what was potentially my first home purchase. I remember taking a student that I was mentoring at the time with me to expose him to the process of buying a home and all that is involved in becoming a first-time homeowner. Two days before the showing, I researched the pricing of other houses in the area, when the home was built, who the previous owners were, and the demographics of the area.

We arrived at the home at around 2:07 PM for an appointment scheduled for 2:15 PM so we could see the surrounding area, possibly meet the neighbors, and get acclimated to the neighborhood. Whether you are buying a house, a car, or making any other large investment doing YOUR OWN research beforehand is the difference between the purchase of good house and a great house, making an acceptable deal or an exceptionally remarkable deal, and seeing a 3.5% increase in annual wealth or maybe a 13.5% increase in annual wealth. It is vital that you first gain knowledge and a holistic understanding of what you are spending YOUR money on. You need to know if a venture is feasible for you and aligns with where you want to be financially and personally in the future. Too many people give their money to so-called investors to invest and just trust that person to be a professional in their field. In many cases, victims of fraud spend more money after the fact than they would have had they spent just a little more time up front investigating and making a better financial decision.

This leads me to the major part of this chapter and a major key in not only business but also your personal and professional success as an individual. It doesn't matter if you're a veteran in business, a seasoned entrepreneur, someone who aspires to own a business, or a student trying to find your niche. I cannot stress enough how important it is to understand the product you are investing in. In my experience with the realtor, there was a clear inconsistency with what I read online about her firm, all their notable accomplishments, her knowledge of the home that she was attempting to sell me, and the surrounding area. I asked questions about the demographics, the surrounding area and potential resale value, and asked why the owners wanted to sell the home. These were questions that I had already researched online and knew the answers to, but I wanted to see the competency and expertise of the realtor to gain more insight on her personal experience since she was selling the home. Bill Birnbach quoted, "Know your product inside and out before you start working. And relate that knowledge to the consumer's needs."

It doesn't matter if you're in automotive, real estate, technological sales, sole proprietorship, or inspirational or motivational speaking, you must understand your business and the product you're selling. If you are trying to start a business, here are ten things to understand and take the initiative in doing to turn feasible ideas into successful businesses. We will discuss some of them in depth.

The Ten Golden Nuggets

1. Write all your ideas on paper.
2. Scope out your industry.
3. Study your competition.
4. Who is your consumer/client?
5. What is it that you are selling? And, why?
6. Start to think about funding/financial burden.
7. Refine the concept.
8. Seek advice from friends, peers, mentors, and industry professionals.
9. Scrap the business plan and just do it.
10. Come back and build a strong business model based on your experience.

Write your ideas and dreams.

In Dillard University's 2015 graduation commencement speech, award-winning actor Denzel Washington stated, "A dream without goals only fuels disappointment." His statement stuck with me. Everything you think, dream, talk about, and hope for means nothing unless you take the first step, put it on paper, and begin to set goals towards making it a reality. Les Brown, a global motivational speaker, stated, "The wealthiest place in the world is in the graveyard." When I first heard this, I said to myself, "Hmmm. That doesn't even make sense." But the more I thought about it, the more I saw the validity in his statement. The graveyard is full of people who died with ideas never put into action, potential never realized, and dreams never made into reality. Additionally, there a lot of people who died with doubt and disappointment. So, I challenge you to put your ideas into action. Learn the lan-

THE MISSION PLAN: THE DECISION

guage, build the app, and change the community. It all starts with you realizing the potential and putting it on paper. Don't trust your memory! A dull pencil beats a sharp mind any day. Put those dreams, goals, and game-changing ideas down on paper.

Scope out your industry.

The definition of SCOPE in business would be known as a project management term that is a combination of objectives and requirements ultimately necessary to complete a project at a given time. Understanding the scope of your project, yourself or your industry allows you, the CEO, to gather an estimation of the true validity of your project, feasibility of your idea, and the time required to finish the project. When scoping out the industry, you want to gather all the information and deliverables that are expected to first understand your market, but first see where you can be competitively advantageous. Too many people run into problems and waste time, resources, and ultimately money because they don't research their industry and do not understand what is considered a need vs. a want to targeted users, customers, or clients. If what you are creating is for your use only then so be it, but if you plan on creating something for others, you want to create what the market and the customer needs.

If we want to align the scope of the project with you being and becoming the CEO of you, there must be a level understanding of self before you can truly be the person you were meant to be. How do you expect to sell a product when you can't even sell yourself? How do you expect to get hired for a new position if you cannot explain what you contributed to your previous position or what you learned from that experience? I want you to understand that many lessons we learn in life are transferable to business; everything is interconnected. If you do not know how to deal with problems when they arise among your peers and you lean towards violence during disagreements or conflict, how can an employer trust that you will be able to handle yourself appropriately in the workplace when your team may disapprove or disagree with your ideas? If your close friends and family view you as an untrustworthy person who cannot be trusted to keep quiet about confidential information, how can an employer trust you with sensitive financial, human resource-related documents, government material that may come in. How can they ensure that you won't sell their secrets to competition or foreign entities? Or, if you have a habit of showing up to events late without informing others, how can your employer trust you to be on time? Certain habits that we have in our personal lives can impact us in the workplace.

Many of us believe that being a businessman or businesswoman is a special privilege with a special set of rules and protocols we must learn to be successful in business. However, what they didn't teach you in that business class, or during that MBA, is that business success begins with personal success. You cannot truly be successful in business until you get it together within your personal life. I am not saying that everything must be completely together in your life and 100% organized at home, however, a lot of what we naturally do flows over into how we will handle or deal with situations within the work setting.

Study your competition.

I am an advocate of just going out and doing it in business instead of all the planning, writing, strategizing, and analyzing. I believe that the time that it takes to plan, write, strategize, etc. is time taken away from the actual marketplace. I want to touch on the theory of the business plan before we discuss how it affects YOU daily. Understanding and knowing who you are competing within business and what they are offering can be the key to leading a company successfully or watching your hard work fall apart. Having this knowledge will enable you to strategically set your prices to compete in the market and help you to quickly respond to economic factors that occur in the marketplace. This knowledge of your competitors will allow you to create a marketing strategy that will help you to take advantage of their weaknesses and sharpen your business model based upon their strengths.

I remember having a conversation with a good friend of mine about his potential business endeavors. After he told me his idea, I asked him about his potential competitors. He responded that the timing was perfect because there were no competitors in the marketplace for his idea.

Competition is not specific to just the type of business idea you have. Even if your movie theater or nightclub is the only one in town, you still have to compete with the other sources of entertainment available in the area. All businesses face competition, either direct or indirect. With globalization and the new technological push with e-commerce, we are no longer just competing with our neighboring businesses or industries. Our competitors could be located anywhere in the world. In Daymond John's book, "The Brand Within," he discusses that a lot of ideas are not innovative or new, they have just been leveraged in unique ways, and the idea has been marketed to fit the need of the consumers. But, you will not know how to market, leverage, or capitalize on weaknesses if you do not understand your competition. Your competition is not just another business taking money away from you or your company. Understanding your competition, means knowing to the best of your ability about specific products or services that are being developed in the future that you may need to sell or consider patenting or licensing before somebody snatches up the idea.

Who are your customers?

Knowing your competition plays a critical part in business success, but another major component is understanding your customer base. One of the biggest misconceptions or errors entrepreneurs make is that they create products they want or have a need for versus creating products that fit the basic needs of our consumers. American author, entrepreneur, marketer, and public speaker, Seth Godin, quoted, "Don't find customers for your products, find products for your customers." It doesn't matter how good your product or service may be, if your consumers don't want it or believe they need it, they will not buy what you are selling. It doesn't matter how good your selling techniques, marketing gimmicks, or even incentives are, if customers do not want or need to buy what you are offering, they won't buy it. It is very important that you have a clear understanding of what customers want.

For example, let's say you want to establish a restaurant in the small town that you reside in because there are not many restaurants in town that serve quality food. Since you live there, you know that the most popular places are the burger joints and the Mexican restaurant located at two opposite ends of the town. So, you talk with some folks, share your idea, and ask what kind of restaurant they would want and get the preferences of various ones in town. You first gather this market research by sending a written survey to your friends via cell phone text messages and through email. Requests for several different types of restaurants come back, but consistently across the board, the type of restaurant that everyone would love to have in town is Italian. You also want to find out what price point the residents are interested in, whether they would like something a bit more upscale but affordable or a median to low-priced place for date nights and a location where they can feel welcomed on any day of the week.

You have taken the time to collect this research, and the information you've pulled together is proving more and more that the Italian restaurant is the best decision moving forward. Even though you remember the last experience you had with Italian food, and how it made you sick for a week, you must still make a decision based on what the people want. In business, it may be cliché, but putting the customer first is your priority. Putting the customer first, in simple terms, means that a business puts the needs and requirements of a customer ahead of anything and everything else. These types of organizations do the small things that in turn make massive impacts on organizational success. Paying special attention and emphasizing on putting customer's priorities before your own contributes to the business providing personalized customer experiences. Check out these nine tips for becoming more customer-focused:

9 Steps to Becoming More Customer Focused

1. Ask What the Customer Wants
2. Give Your Customer What They Want
3. Ensure Customer Gets What They Want
4. Deliver on Promises
5. Acknowledge Customers
6. Reward Customers
7. Allow Customers to Give Feedback
8. Make Customer Focus a part of Company Culture
9. Change with Time

Why are you selling this product? What is the purpose?

If you aspire to be successful, I have a specific model that will turn all your future dreams into a present reality. I was reading a book once by Simon Sinek called Start with Why, and he talked about leadership being an internal process starting with defining your why or defining that purpose. He went on to talk about the process, and the product and how they are predicted by first defining your purpose. I believe that in success, we can follow that same model. I call it, The 3 Ps to Perfection:

The Purpose
The Process
The Product

Have you ever asked yourself why you wanted to be successful? Aside from the obvious monetary reasons, what drives you to want more out of life? When you begin to define the why, you are moving into the first P, and that is purpose. You're moving into the overall reason for doing something. Understanding your purpose will help you to exhibit the attitude, resiliency, and work ethic you need to be successful. Purpose will energize you to stay up late and wake up early. Purpose is the internal process that people don't see that sets the foundation for the product the world purchases in the future.

Once you establish your purpose, move your steps forward into the process. I look at the process as the GPS. When you type an address or location into your GPS, it will provide you with directions to get to your destination. Along the way, you may run into a traffic jam, have to take a detour because a road is closed, or have to slow down because an accident may occur. Though your direction, speed, and even transportation may change, you cannot change the destination. Understanding your purpose will help you understand that the process is always necessary. In our lives, things, people, support, resources, and our feelings about what we are doing will change. We will experience trials and tribulation. Instead of changing your destination, you must understand how to turn mistakes into monuments of success, trials into triumph, and tribulation into testimonies of how far you've come. In order to be successful, you must train your mind to properly see the process and how it contributes to your purpose. Everything you endure is only a party of the journey necessary to make your dreams come true. Don't look at the processes of life as a loss of time or resources. Use each obstacle as a learning opportunity to grow.

The process is ultimately the implementation plan and strategy to get through your obstacles so you can still get to your destination. The process is where many people fail because it requires the most time and work. This may be cliché, but what you put in is what you get out. If you are putting negative thoughts into your head like, "I can't. I shouldn't. I am not ready. I'm not smart enough. I am too young. Or, I don't have enough money." Then you won't see success. The negativity that goes in stays in, however positivity that goes in blossoms out. When you begin to believe in yourself, trust the process, and put that work in over and over again, no matter the roadblocks, mistakes, or traffic jams, you will become resilient. Resilient people become successful. It may take a little longer to get to than planned to get to your destination, but that is okay! Destinations should never change, but sometimes, the routes to get there have to. Once you have successfully followed the process, then you become a product of the product.

The product is the result. The product in business is the profit, and the product in life is success. You are that something that has been grown and made, equipped with knowledge, sculpted by your experiences, and prepared to be a high performer. You are ready for that last shot to win the game in the fourth quarter, to take that last exam to graduate college, and even to take that company public that has been so successful. If you learn your purpose, map out your implementation plan during the process, you will become the product of the product.

RAW KEYS TO SUCCESS

Have you ever searched everywhere for your keys only to find them in your pocket? After realizing your keys were with you the entire time, you were probably upset about the time you spent turning everything upside down and inside out. Many people experience this in their lives as well. They try every success and life coaching program, only to find that what they needed was on the inside of them the entire time. The keys to life, success, happiness, joy, and fulfillment are already in your pocket waiting for you to make them a part of your life, a component in your decisions, and a switch to your success.

We will focus on resilience, authenticity, and work ethic (RAW). Something raw is unique, authentic, and in its purest form. In order to achieve success in every area of your life, you must embrace the truest, most authentic, and most natural part of yourself. Let's start with resilience. Plainly put, resilience is about your ability not to give up. If you have enough of it, you'll bounce back after ever fall, come back for more after every hit, and try again when you fail. Those who are resilient may experience many knockdowns, a lack of finances, making bad decisions, and even major loss, but they will continue to fight with everything in them. Resilient people look at every failure, disappointment, and let down as a lesson, not a loss. I know what people say, "You win some, you lose some." However, the resilient know that this mindset is flawed. Instead, they believe, "You win some, you learn the rest." Michael Jordan once quoted, "I never lost a game, I just didn't have enough time." To increase your resilience, you must adopt this very mindset.

Understanding and valuing your authenticity is critical. When we compare ourselves to others instead of appreciating what makes us different, we ruin relationships, friendships, and even businesses. In a world where people change their entire lives to follow trends, be unique and distinctly great! It's time to stop trying to fit in and be okay with standing out. You owe it to yourself, your family, and your future accomplishments to be authentic. So, how does one go about building an authentic personal and professional brand? Focus on three areas, your performance, your image, and your exposure.

- Perform well in everything you do. If you are going to put part of your effort in, don't do it. Push yourself to give your best to everything that you put your hands to.
- Ensure that your image is authentic. Yes, I wore suits my senior year, but that is what I desired to do so that I could be taken seriously as a businessman. I don't care what other people in your area of expertise are doing. Don't be afraid to stand out and be uniquely you. Your attire, attitude, morals, and values all play a role in your image. Make sure that when people see you, they see YOU.
- Expose your abilities and impact to people, businesses, and organization. It doesn't matter if you're good if no one knows it. Don't be afraid to put yourself out there.

The final key is your work ethic. You have to out work, out grind, outperform, and out match EVERYONE you are competing against. Every time you hit your target, you must raise the bar, and hit it again. Without work, your dreams remain dreams, and your ideas remain ideas. These three keys have always been in your pocket. Now that you've found them, what do you plan to do with them?

ADVICE TO ADVANCEMENT

Talk is cheap, but great advice can be priceless. Whether it is a business leader answering your specific questions, a peer doing a review of your term paper for grammatical errors, or a potential customer previewing an idea, you can accomplish more with good advice. While we can truly learn something from everyone, we must be certain to take away the right things from the right people. Receiving advice plays a big part in leadership and decision making. You will never have all the answers, and your idea is not the best it can be. We all need the input of others. I have learned so much from others by simply observing and asking questions. I contribute 80% of my success to the advice, leadership, wisdom, and knowledge I have gained from others, and the other 20% to the actual execution of what they said. Yes, listening and execution play a major role. My dad always used the familiar saying, "You can lead a horse to water, but you cannot make him drink." And that is so true in business. Advice means absolutely nothing if you do not put it into action. Failing to heed the advice you asked for and received is a complete waste of your time and theirs.

A fruitful exchange means that both individuals benefit in some way. This may not be monetary, but the person giving the advice should at least feel appreciated for sharing their wisdom. I believe that information is one of the most influential things we can receive in business. Gathering the right information at the right time with the right execution plan can give you a definite competitive advantage over your competition. Sometimes, benefits as large as positioning your company for large investments, or as innocuous as being introduced to someone who could complement the project you are working on. Regardless of how large or small the advantage, you must always be ready to receive and implement the right information.

Understand that when you are seeking information, you can't just go around asking anyone and expecting them to tell you everything you want to know. Everyone's advice isn't good advice. More so, just because it's good advice doesn't mean it's good advice for you, your brand, or your goals. This is where selecting good mentors come into play. Talk with those closest to you and build on those great organic relationships with people who care about you, add value to your life, and contribute to your long-term success.

JUST DO IT

Nike coined the slogan "Just Do It" in 1988. Weirdly enough, it was inspired by Gary Gilmore, a spree-killer who was sentenced to death for murdering two people. When asked if he had any final words before his execution, Gary Gilmore stated, "Let's do it." Though these were Gilmore's final words, they inspired a slogan that continues to represent one of the most successful athletic shoe companies in the world and inspire people all across the globe. These three words, just do it, will turn your dreams into reality. They represent the final step in any developmental process. All your thoughts, research, ideas, and plans mean absolutely nothing without action. Do not blame your lack of progress on your lack of finances, staff, or location and don't let your current circumstances limit you. If you don't have the finances for your project, go make the money, find the money, or borrow the money. If you don't have the time to get the work done, associate yourself with people who will add value to your vision and build a team. If you do not have the infrastructure, well, Google, Microsoft, and Apple started in a garage, so, why can't you? Put your thoughts and plans into action where you are with what you have.

Maybe those three words don't inspire you as much as they inspire me. It doesn't matter where you get your inspiration, just find the necessary amount to get off the couch, stop scrolling on social media, and make your dreams into realities. It's time for your ideas to become innovations and your how into NOW. You can think out your plan over and over again, but actual industry experience will help you gain the knowledge and insight you need to grow your company and learn your customer base. What you read online and in books and information from advisors are often based upon opinion and not fact. Facts are best gained through experience. You must chase the facts and based on the facts, you make the adjustments and changes needed to improve your business. However, none of this will happen if you don't start somewhere.

OBSERVATION PLAN

In the previous sections, we discussed the importance of information. In this section, I will show you how to use every bit of information you gain to improve your business. Business plans are great. In business school, they teach all about the importance and value of having a business plan. While I understand the need for business plans at some point in any business, I would like to share some information about what I call an observation plan. The primary purpose of an observation plan is to lead your company to success based on experience, observation, and information you have gathered in your real-life experience. Many of my associates in corporate America have said that the best training is on the job training. I believe the best business plans are based on the industry's experiences, customer interactions, and economic factors. You cannot build something tangible and sustainable based on research and ideas alone. You build it by leveraging your experience, mistakes, and failures as learning opportunities.

After you have gotten through steps 1-9 you will be ready for step 10, which is to continue to execute your observation plan and stick to the steps based upon what you have seen in the industry. If you followed the steps correctly, you now have a formal statement and mission, you have set core company values, you know why they are attainable, and you have the action plans for reaching them. You have information on your competitors, customers, and even ways to generate capital. You have done the actual work and refined the concept and have reinserted the necessary information about the organization in your attempt to reach those goals. You have your observation plan, and you are ready to go!

THE MISSION PLAN: THE DECISION

For this challenge, you'll need access to the internet and some great books. Head to your local library or somewhere quiet. Use your journal or notebook to complete the following activities.

1. Research the ten most successful people, products, or companies in your field of interest.
2. Build a profile on each of them and do a SWOT (Strengths, Weaknesses, Opportunities, & Threats) Analysis
3. Analyze them and identify their weaknesses.
4. Develop a plan of action to make their weaknesses your strengths. What studies should you conduct? What research do you need? Who should you ask for advice? What changes should you implement?
5. Divide your plan into daily, weekly, monthly, and yearly goals.
6. Change your daily routine to align with your goals.
7. Manage your time, accomplish your goals, and live out your dreams.

TIPS FOR SUCCESS

Whatever you feed your mind is how your life will be. Remember, positive in, positive out!

Learn from the mistakes of others and make them your strengths.

Set reasonable goals. (Not too high where you can become discouraged, and not too low where they become boring.) Challenge your mind, transform your life, and begin to accomplish your goals.

TAKE A CPC (consistency, persistence, confidence) PILL. Build your confidence, stay committed to your dreams, and be persistent in making them a reality. Stop making excuses! The time is now!

"Starve your distractions and feed your focus."
— Charmaine Hayden

CHAPTER FIVE
NOW, WHAT'S STOPPING YOU?

One day, I was having dinner with a friend of mine. As I updated her on my life, upcoming travel, and new endeavors, she began to cry. I thought I might have said something that offended her, so I quickly asked what I'd done and if she was okay. She went on to explain that she had been through a rough patch in life. She felt like her life was meaningless and that she never wanted to get to a place in her life where all she did was work a regular 9 to 5 job. At the time, she was a recent college graduate, and a week away from starting work with Boeing, the number one defensive contractor in the world. She explained how nothing she was doing aligned with her purpose and how she felt she had so many things keeping her from her purpose. She was frustrated and depressed about taking the job with Boeing and where she was in life. After she had talked for a while, I gently interrupted her to ask two questions: Where do you want to be in life? What's stopping you?

THE MISSION PLAN: THE DECISION

Here's what she responded:

> "What's stopping me, is me! I am my own worst enemy. I never see the good in me because no matter how nice I try to be to people, I'm always the one being talked about or made fun of. I know things could have always been worse, but to me, it's bad enough not being not accepted and feeling like I don't have a place in this world. I have never fit in completely, and I could never truly be myself. I could never speak up for myself. My "friends" all walked away. I thought I was an important part of the group, but I wasn't. People have always been my problem, people were the ones I wanted to please most, and they were the ones I wanted to like me.
>
> So, all in all, I have been trying to recover myself my entire life thus far. I have always let fear and me not thinking I would be good enough stop me, or even the thought of just failing."

Silence filled the room, tears were running down her face, and the tissues were piling up beside her. Full of pain, disappoint, and anger she looked up and said to me, "See, I just don't feel like I'm strong enough to get through this." I handed her a sheet of paper and a pencil and asked her to write all of her accomplishments to date and the position that she is in. Here's what she wrote:

1. I was an Honor Roll Student all four years of college
2. I was on Dean's list all four years of college
3. I gained internships with Toyota, Brookhaven, USACE,

and had the opportunity to study abroad in Germany.
4. I was the first in my family to graduate college with a bachelor's degree
5. I graduated college at the top of my class and received an offer from Boeing at their headquarters office
6. I bought a brand-new car with my own money
7. I pay all my bills and have no debt

As I read what she wrote down, I was amazed. I learned so much that night and realized that so many others feel the same way. The fact is that many people allow their past situations and circumstances to put them in a place of present limitation. So many people let others dictate their happiness, joy, and destiny. Many people don't know how to be positive in every instance and wholeheartedly believe that circumstances will get better.

In my early years, I was that person. I had awesome plans for others, great advice, and wisdom in various situations. I was the friend you could call on in times of desperation but I felt as if there was no one I could call on when I was in need. I had addictions that I couldn't seem to break, insecurities that I couldn't seem to strengthen, and doubts that I couldn't seem to overcome. I was in a position where I had violent thoughts, thoughts of running away, and even thoughts of committing suicide. I hated myself because I never took the time to learn myself, get to know myself, and in life, it is very hard to love something or someone you don't know or aren't familiar with. I looked at life as an obligation and never as an opportunity. I let others dictate my decisions and influence who I was as a person, from the clothes I wore, to the music I listened to, to

THE MISSION PLAN: THE DECISION

the places I went, and the friends I associated with. I was too busy being "cool" than being complete and I couldn't ever face the man in the mirror because I was focused on the next trend. But it wasn't until I started to understand that I came in this world as an individual, to stand out and not fit in, that I began to discover that I was worth more than anyone's rumors, any job's salary, and what anyone thought I was. I soon began to realize that if I wanted anything great out of life, I had to change the way I perceived it.

The fact that you are reading this book, living, breathing, and are still in good health regardless of everything that has happened to you is proof that God has allowed you to accomplish so much over the years. Before we can receive blessings of success, we have to understand how to remain grateful through the struggle. Take the time in every negative situation, to see the positive and look for an opportunity to make it better. Take time out of your day and your every-day life to see the positive in yourself and stop letting others influence your emotions, your mind, decisions, success, and your destiny.

We've made it to the final chapter, and I must say, I've truly enjoyed our journey. You've made it this far because you have been learning something, you are reading the information you can relate to, or you truly want to be successful. For a moment, I want you to think about this question: What has kept you from experiencing success in every area of your life? I know you are probably thinking this question would have been more befitting at the beginning of the book. However, as we come to the end of our first of many journeys together, I want to remind you of the only thing that can keep you from success. Right now, it is the only thing holding you back from taking the steps to become that entrepreneur, lawyer, or doctor. It's the only reason why you haven't finished that book, or asked for your girlfriend's hand in marriage. No, it is not your finances, or a lack thereof. It is not your age. You are not too young or too old to continue to live out your dreams. Your weight is not stopping you from running that marathon or being a successful model. Your girlfriend, your parents, spouse, nor children are keeping you from making your dreams a reality. The only barricade stopping you from crossing the bridge of opportunity is the person you see when you look into the mirror.

The power of you is so powerful, amazing, and magnificent. Understanding the true power that is within you is exhilarating. We experience freedom like none other when we come to understand that we are the only ones who determine how high we can go. During an interview I listened to, both Bill Gates and Warren Buffet were asked to explain one thing that contributed to their wealth of success. They both answered with one word, FOCUS. Focus is the state or quality of having or producing clear visual definition. Or, the center of interest or activity. What we focus on determines where we will invest our time, money, skills, and resources. This generation has made the environment, social media, and even fashion trends the main focus. For this reason, we have a bunch of socially conscious well-dressed individuals who are bold enough to use their social media platforms to address every issue that arrives, but too lazy to get up and do something about it. Sometimes, we lose focus because of what we view as failure or disappointment. Trust me, I understand. When

THE MISSION PLAN: THE DECISION

things don't go as planned or when life throws an unexpected blow, it is sometimes hard to stay afloat or stay focused. In too many cases, people talk about failure, fill their minds with negativity and think only of the worst possible outcome. As a result, they give up and find something "easier" to focus on. If Steve Jobs gave up after his third or fourth phone call to angel investors to invest in early Apple technology, there would be no Apple as we know it today. If Michael Jordan had given up the first time he was cut from his high school basketball team, the way we look at athletic sneakers and basketball would be very different.

Instead of changing your focus, learn how to turn trials and tribulations into telescopes you can use to remain focused. I want you to learn how to turn those disappointments into decisions to solve problems and become generational cycle breakers. And ultimately, I want you to learn how to turn those mistakes into monuments towards your success.

Colonel Harland Sanders was one of the most courageous men of the twentieth century. He accomplished great things and defied all odds stacked against him. At the age of five, his father passed away, and his life from that point on was filled with sorrow and disappointment. At the age of 16, he quit school and by the age of 17, he had lost four jobs because of his anger and lack of commitment. He was married at the age of 18 and for four years, worked as a railroad conductor, eventually failing at this endeavor as well. This gentleman then went on to join the army and washed. Colonel aspired to go to law school, but when he was rejected, that dream became another failure. During his time as a railroad conductor, he had his first child, a young daughter. At the age of 20, his wife took their daughter away from him because of the bad influence he had on her. Fast forward some years to age 65, when he retired and received his first retirement check of $105.00. In his eyes, that check said that he couldn't provide for himself. The next year, he couldn't deal with his life anymore, decided to commit suicide, but failed drastically – again. One day, he sat under a tree to write his will, however, he began to write what he wished he would have accomplished in life instead. He then realized, at the age of 68, that the only thing he could do better than anyone was cook. So, Colonel Sanders borrowed $87 against his retirement check, bought and fried some chicken using his own special recipe, and went door to door to sell them to his neighbors throughout Kentucky. The same man who tried to commit suicide, lost both of his parents early on in life, faced countless hardships and struggles, and failed more times than he could count became the founder of what is now a billion-dollar fast-food restaurant chain, Kentucky Fried Chicken. Because he stayed committed, true, and focused his attitude on what he was called to do, KFC went on to become one of the first American fast food chains to go international and is now one of the world's largest restaurant chains. Imagine that!

I am a firm believer that failure, is simply success in its earliest form. Some of the success I have seen personally comes from the belief that I have in myself and not allowing my fear to get in the way or cause me to take action that is not aligned with my dreams. Everyone wants followers on social media. Everyone wants likes on their statuses or pictures. Everyone wants views on their videos. However, not everyone has a clear-cut vision of what they want in their lives. When people talk about visions, it is like it is a supernatural feeling, like a fairy tale or a form of magic. But it isn't. Visions are real. You are the vision every day you wake up. You are the visionary and your actions, the decisions you make, the experiences that you go through, the things you talk about, the things you eat, and the people that you associate your life with are all a part of your vision. The vision is the person you want to become, or the person you are becoming. You live your vision every single day. With actions, investments of time, resources, relationships, and friendships, you map out your vision every day. Every second or minute wasted, are seconds taken away from the time where you can be creating. You are the driver, pilot, and captain of your life. The question is: Where are you going? What is the vision for your life? And what are you doing about it? Align your thoughts, actions, and feet toward what you want to see.

Some years ago, I had a conversation with a close friend of mine about her finances. She told me how she wanted to get out of debt and complained about her financial situation. She had just graduated from college and was about to start a new position soon. She went on and on about how she didn't know how to invest, she didn't have extra money to save, and she had accumulated a great deal of debt in the form of credit cards, student loans, and other bills. As I listened, she never mentioned the things she did for herself – not once. She didn't talk about taking herself to a movie, getting her nails done, or going away for a weekend beach trip. She was living to pay bills; she wasn't really living.

Many of you are going through some of the same things that the MAJORITY of Americans are going through today.

Most are either in debt, don't know how to save, don't know where to invest, or may have never had the proper training or coaching to become financially responsible. A recent study showed that 8 out of 10 people, 80% of the American population is in debt of some kind. Whether it is credit card expenses, an overdue phone bill, a car note, or student loans, unpaid debt can be crippling.

It is important that you understand that you must invest in the vision you have for your life. When you are hungry, you owe it to yourself to get something to eat, however, instead of picking something up in the drive-thru, line, or to-go counter, you have an opportunity to spend a little extra time and less money by going to the grocery store and buying fresh produce and a good cut of meat to prepare a healthy meal for yourself. You now have benefited your pocketbook by saving money and benefited your body by eating a healthy meal. You now have leftovers that can serve as additional meals for later in the week vs. fast food which would have only satisfied your craving for food for thirty minutes. That one decision can prove to be either an investment in you or an expense to you. If we find ways to multiply instead of decline, we will be successful financially, spiritually, mentally, emotionally, and maybe even physically. Everything you do must be an INVESTMENT in your vision, and NOT an Expense.

The difference between an investment and an expense is simple: one will pay you back, and the other will drain your resources. When we talk about resources, they don't always have to be financial or tangible. Your resources can be your time, your emotions, and even your mental capabilities. Stop for a moment and ask yourself this question: Have you ever given your time and energy to someone who drained you mentally, emotionally, and physically, and turned out to be a complete waste of your time? If you're at least 18, I'll assume the answer is yes. Now, ask yourself this: How much more positive and productive could that time have been if you had spent it with someone who supported your dreams, was a loyal friend to you, or truly added value to your life? Put your funds, your mind, and your time into activities and people that make a better return on YOUR LIFE investment.

THE POWER OF SAYING NO

Earlier this year I finished a book by Greg McKeown entitled, Essentialism: The Disciplined Pursuit of Less. The book teaches readers how to get more done in less time. One of his concepts empowered me to have a systematic discipline for discerning what is absolutely essential, then eliminating everything that is not; in turn, I am now able to make the highest possible contribution towards the things that really matter.

How many times have you said yes to someone or something just because you didn't want to disappoint them by saying no? Times at work when you are already overwhelmed by projects, you continue to say yes to more projects and then wonder why your performance is lacking. In a social relationship you know you are trying to reach a financial savings goal but you continue to say yes to every opportunity to go out and enjoy the weekends. Or even those times when you went out on a weekday because you didn't want your friend to go alone when you knew you had to finish studying for the final exam the next day. I've been a victim of all three of these examples, saying yes to everything because I feared the outcome of "no." When did the word "no" become so bad to say, and a word that is so hardly used?

Still, for so many people, it can be very challenging to know how to set boundaries for their lives or the simple act of saying "no" to others. I want to provide a few important things to consider that will help in your pursuit of mastering "NO."

Accept the emotional backlash.

In the past, I would fear to say no because of the emotional backlash from other people. I would always think they were going to get mad or they may get disappointed because I was my unwillingness to join the festivities. In my experience, I thought people would judge me, dislike me, or reject me by just saying no to the partying, social events, or even opportunities at work. I've learned over time that people do the exact opposite by respecting you and valuing your decisions. Remember this, the people who you want to surround yourself with are those who will respect your boundaries, even if initially they feel upset or disappointed.

Put YOU First.

When you say yes to others, you have to be sure that you are not saying no to yourself, your dreams, and no to your destiny. You have to make the decision to become a priority in your life. Before you give your all your compassion, all your love, and all your support to others, don't forget to apply that same love, compassion, and support towards yourself.

You deserve the best, you deserve the world, and you deserve to treat yourself with the same compassion and kindness that you continue to give to others. What works for me may not work for you but I recommend you set aside some time weekly to take care of yourself. During this time, it gives you the ability to relax, reset, and recharge your batteries.

THE ESSENTIALS OF SETTING BOUNDARIES

Setting boundaries are critical to your overall sense of well being and are an important part of having healthy relationships. When you begin to set boundaries, it doesn't just free up space in your mind and on your calendar, it redirects the energy to the things that truly excite and motivate you. Having boundaries enables you to experience less stress while you focus on living your life's true purpose.

Growing up, I let so many different people run my life, emotions, decisions, and actions. I was never focused on the essentials or a specific priority because I was trying to fit everything into my schedule, live a life full of pleasing everyone else, and became overwhelmed, less productive and frustrated all of the time. I wasn't the one that was just suffering, the quality of my work suffered as well. When I learned how to "JUST SAY NO," it silenced the noise, it cleared my plate of unmet expectations and minimized my stress levels.

Beginning today, it's time for you to stand up, protect your boundaries, and say only yes to the essential things in life. Stop getting distracted by the things that have nothing to do with your goals, your dreams, and destiny.

Pull out your notebook or journal and answer the following questions.

1. What value is this decision bringing to my life?
2. How will my actions this make me a better person?
3. What are my top priorities in life?
4. Where's most of my time going?
5. Are my decisions my decisions or are they influenced by other factors?
6. What brings me the most happiness?

TIPS FOR SUCCESS

Don't be afraid to put yourself first.

No is a complete sentence. You don't owe an explanation for your priorities.

You owe it to yourself to be financially, mentally, emotionally, and physically healthy!

Remember that failure is only success in its early stage.

What we focus on determines where we will invest our time, money, skills, and resources.

SECTION TWO

THE DISCOVERY

In our last journey, we left off discussing investments and expenses. My friend, I hope that in this book, you will come to understand that your future currency is generated by the investments you make today. Your investments in time, resources, money, and even energy matter greatly. During this discovery phase, you will be taught how to create opportunities during times of opposition. You will leverage your trials and tribulations as a testimony towards your path of success. You will learn the importance of asking, "What can I learn from this experience?" The true power of self-realization and revelation of your natural gifts and talents is the knowledge that will accelerate you into the abyss of achievement and inner confidence. In this volume, you will be led to discover your unique talents, natural gifts, and how to enjoy yourself as you enter into a timeless awareness of self. Your prior state of disbelief will become a state of bliss as you discover your divinity, master your unique talents, and are empowered by servicing others.

MIRACLES

What is growth without change?
What is success without pain?
What is life without sacrifice?
Are your dreams keeping you up at night?
Are your skies still blue?
Is your water still clear?
Stop waiting for a miracle; you already know what to do.
The gifts are outside
The knowledge is in your mind
The passion is in your heart
You've had it since the beginning; it's just been waiting for you to start.
Let your soul become free.
Let your skin become tough.
You're already fit to overcome obstacles, hurdle tribulations, and walk through the rough.
Bow your head and believe.
Don't let your doubt deceive.
Begin to plant the seeds,
Let the rain harvest your plants.
Let the growth become even clearer.
The miracle has always been right there…
When you consider the mirror.

"The purpose of life is to contribute in some way to making things better."

– Robert F. Kennedy

INTRODUCTION
MAKE A DIFFERENCE

Before you begin to read the next few sentences, I want you to ask yourself aloud, "Who am I?" You will either sit there with a smile, happy about your accomplishments, drop your head in confusion because you are not quite sure, or, you will feel disappointment when you think of who you have become.

Whether you have helped thousands with your medical talents, lived a mediocre life trying to find yourself as an individual, or have sinned for the selfishness of your appetites, the knowledge compiled in this chapter will give you a better understanding of the realities of the world. I assure you that upon reading the last word in closing, the answer you gave just now will change and you will transform.

The term family as we know it, in my opinion, is indeed deeper than bloodline. Looking at the global spectrum, the importance and structure of families have truly changed. According to a study done by the Pew Research Center in December of 2015, the dominant family structure has died, and "parents today are raising their children against a backdrop of increasingly diverse and for many, constantly evolving family forms." In 1960, two-parent households dominated families. By 2014, two-parent households only made up 46% of families. As the number of two-parent households continues to decline, one-parent households increased from 9% in 1960 to 26% just a few decades later.

> [The living arrangements of black children stand in stark contrast to the other major racial and ethnic groups. The majority – 54% – are living with a single parent. Just 38% are living with two parents, including 22% who are living with two parents who are both in their first marriage. Some 9% are living with remarried parents, and 7% are residing with parents who are cohabiting.]
>
> - Pew Research Center, December 2015

So, we ask ourselves, is this new society conducive for the reality of all? Or, are our actions subject to our extinction? During my junior summer in undergrad at Alabama A&M University (AAMU) I was among a group selected to go to Ghana, Africa to obtain knowledge in our respective majors and put together a project that would contribute to our future career fields. The goal was to get an international experience that we would take back to AAMU and share it with culture, knowledge, and friendship. Weeks leading up to my trip, it didn't sink in that I was going to be leaving the country for the first time in my life. I had become very level-headed; I wouldn't let anything get me excited until it happened. When my friends asked about my excitement for the trip to Ghana, all I could say was, "I mean it has not hit me yet, but yes, it is going to be a great experience." I sat there and smiled in my arrogance, selfishness, and lack of appreciation of everything that I was ahead of me. Before I left, I received many calls from my family and friends saying how proud they were and how they looked forward to talking to me when I returned so they could be a part of the experience. On June 15, 2013, I wrote the following journal entry:

> "Today is the day before I travel to Accra, Ghana.... first time officially out the country and I will be visiting the mother of earth, Africa. Oh, my goodness, I have so many questions. How will the food be? The people? The women? Will people accept us as Americans or look at us more as kings and queens because they think we are rich? I feel more than appreciative and so very grateful for this once in a lifetime opportunity ahead of me. I would not pass this up for anything, and I plan to take full advantage of it. The craziest part is that it hasn't even hit me yet. Like I am sitting here on my bed, and in 24 hours, I will be en route to Ghana on a plane with three other American students researching in our fields. I absolutely love my life. I truly am blessed and fortunate. This experience will change my life I am sure. That's all I have for tonight. I'm sure there will be much more tomorrow."

Even as I wrote this, I was not nearly as excited as I was weeks after I lived in Ghana for 17 days. Often, we do not appreciate the blessings in front of us. My trip showed me how other cultures long for the things we often take for granted every day such as the water we drink, the air we breathe, and the roads we walk on.

I believe that experience is the best teacher; therefore in this chapter, I will take you through my experiences and guide you through properly reviewing and upgrading your own. My seventeen-day journey in Africa was more than just a trip; it was an encounter that gave me the tools to transform my life and ultimately, the lives of others.

I have always had a strong passion for helping people and truly making a difference in people's lives. But it wasn't until my journey in Ghana that my eyes were opened up to both the true beauties of the world and the terrifying struggles that millions of people endure daily. As I think of the time I spent with my classmates in Africa, a wide and bright smile spreads across my face. Regardless of the many other places I will and have ventured, the sights and sounds of Ghana was an experience that I will carry for the rest of my days. I will forever cherish the memories of going on a safari, surviving the roadway, and even our bus being attacked by a local on the side of the street. Through it all, my classmates and I stood, survived, and learned together. Even further, I do not believe a better scholastic combination could have been selected. Mixing Finance, International Business, Marketing, and Political Science was a perfect combination to promote varying viewpoints about the many experiences we encountered abroad.

Our Ghana experience provided a healthy environment for genuine learning to take place on a global scale. Each day was a mentally engaging and rewarding experience. It is without question that this program changed my viewpoint of Ghana, but even further, it sharpened my focus and piqued my interest in potentially working somewhere on the continent of Africa. I fell in love with the country and continent even more. My soul gained direction, and my life developed an intense yearning to re-engage on the global scale. While in Ghana, it did not matter if I did not have hot water, air conditioning, or reliable Internet because I was in love with the country, people, land, air, and water. I wanted to drink in all the culture I could during my short stay in Ghana. I wanted to feel the heat of the countryside and taste all Ghana's sweet fruits. I would say, I was able to check all those things off of my checklist and I am proud to have done them. I came back to the United States with a blazing appreciation for all the little accommodations, conveniences, and standards I have always enjoyed without every thinking about how life could potentially be without them.

Seeing the ingenuity in the classrooms filled with focused students that were so committed to educational excellence regardless of the lack thereof resources or access to materials was mind-blowing. Upon seeing the student's hunger and thirst for knowledge, I immediately began to think about how many of my cohorts in America skipped class and often grumbled about having to attend. My experience allowed me to witness the professors teach students at a higher standard and instill greatness through an elevated thought process.

They taught students how to critically think and become activists to change their personal and family situations. Learning that it is possible to use education as a tool to fight crime, violence, injustice, and racial inequalities was eye-opening.

These focal points served as the basis of an idea I formulated to create a standing infrastructure that would provide underrepresented students with the necessary skills and resources to become leaders who will tackle global issues. From these experiences, my interest was piqued and I began to research to formulate an understanding. From the understanding I obtained, a creative action plan was devised to tackle the educational injustice and inequalities around our world. I worked relentlessly to create solutions for those who did not grow up into the affluent, middle class family and were unable to provide elite educational support. The SHINE Institute was officially formed in early 2015 with a mission to develop the next generation of globally competitive business leaders through educational excellence and professional development. Following the mission, four core values that would produce a company culture that would last forever.

To Improve
Improve educational and professional possibilities for students in college

To Innovate
Innovate by creating techniques and developing new models of learning to better the traditional standards of achievement and educational excellence

To Impact
Impact communities through community service, entrepreneurship and a heightened awareness of educational excellence

To Inspire
Inspire future leaders by exposing students to various career

opportunities and bridging the gap between the worlds of education and business

It is a beautiful feeling when you can witness your work, that was once a blank canvas, be transformed into an impressive masterpiece designed to transform the lives of all who experience it. I want to take this opportunity to share how you too can turn your future dreams into your current realities. If you don't remember anything from this book, I want you to remember these three things…

1. Embrace Your Failures
2. Be the Hardest Worker
3. Keep a Positive Attitude

After being falsely accused of rape my freshman year of college, many who were once in my corner were no longer allies. I couldn't call on those who once supported me. Quite frankly, they assumed I would succumb to the statistics of the black male in today's society – death or jail. Close family members and friends I grew up with didn't believe in me and thought I couldn't recover. At times, I questioned my strength and wondered if I was even resilient enough to bounce back. I thought about dropping out of school, I had suicidal thoughts, and I questioned my value in this world. The way I saw it, a lot of people would be happier if I just ended my life. Instead of letting my failures extinguish my faith in God's ability to restore me, I embraced my failures, enrolled at Alabama A&M University, and focused on my studies with a dream of being the most successful person to ever graduate from that school. I came in school with focus, determination, and commitment to never let my environment, my circumstance, or even my mistakes break me, but I let them serve as the bridge that would connect me to the next opportunity.

When I got involved in the community and reached out to some of the nearby school systems, I noticed discrepancies and inequalities in the lower-income district compared to the more affluent district. My involvement was never about the bottom-line, it was about making a difference and solving some of the issues that we were facing right in my city. I got a lot of pushback from educators, state officials, and even my parents at the time for many different reasons. They all said things like, "The workload is too much. You are too young and don't have enough experience. You don't have time; you are still a college student."

I never focused on the critics or the negativity. In addition to the commentary in the stands, I had my own issues on the court. I was $7,000 in debt with no steady income coming in and taking an 18-hour course load. I focused on the potential opportunity to corner the market, provide a quality service, and build a social and community presence. It was not about seeing the flowers bloom; it was about putting in the work to plant the seeds.

Once during a lecture, a student raised their hands and asked, "When talking about self, is it bad to mention the negative things first? Even though you understand what you need to work on, cope with, and amend, Is it bad to mention the bad first?" I thought about the student's question for a moment, then immediately changed the direction of the lecture and brought them back to memories when they were children. I gave the students a scenario of a typical day in school. "If the intercom comes on in your classroom, what is the first thought that would go through your mind? Would it be positive or negative?" I asked. Then, I had the students to raise their hands if it was something negative. Out of a classroom of 66 students, 61 raised their hands that they would have a negative thought. I explained to them that this thinking, thought process, and small habits cause us to acknowledge more of the negativity in our lives without rejoicing the positive. Thus, we never become truly satisfied or happy with ourselves, others, or our surroundings. Instead of talking about what we are good at, or who we are trying to become, we only communicate about our imperfections and what we don't have.

The same message that I relayed to the students is the same message I am relaying to you in this book! Focus on your strengths. Put your energy into building your purpose. Work on the skills that were granted to you since birth instead of worrying about things that only appease other people. I was very good at communicating, connecting with people, and networking with people that could potentially serve as liaisons and supporters of the Project SHINE, Inc. Brand. So those are the things I put my energy into. Our focus should be on maximizing strengths, not amending weaknesses, and becoming the best instead of building to be balanced.

Becoming good at something takes time, but becoming the best at anything takes strategy. I tapped into the young professional network and started to learn the marketplace. I understood that there was a paradigm shift happening in Huntsville in the Young Professional Community and they would be great contributors and supporters to my products and services. I knew that if I were into the social community, I would be able to leverage some of the people who were influential in making decisions for the future of the Huntsville Community. I was a student taking six classes (equivalent to 18 credit hours), working 30-40 hours a week at the local BMW dealership, and developing a non-profit organization. Yes, I was a father, an employee, a student, a CEO and a community leader. I was busier than most adults were in the later parts of their careers, and I loved every bit of it. I have learned that if you want something, it is not enough to just work for it. You must plan for it, dream about it, think about it, and ultimately live it. Students often teased me for wearing suits to class every day, but they didn't understand that I was only in class for a small part of my day. Before and after class, I was in business meetings with the movers and shakers of Huntsville to obtain investments and investors for my dreams. My schedule consisted of late nights, early mornings, and even longer days! I never let my stress levels dictate the level I would operate in. I remained positive and focused on the opportunity, not the obligation or the many, many obstacles I had to get through.

Do you think Tenizing Norgay and Edmond Hillary, both New Zealand mountaineers, explorers, and philanthropists quit the first time they fell en route to the top of Mount Everest? No. They took it as an opportunity to get up and keep pushing to the top. They looked up at the top of Mount Everest and knew exactly the level of commitment and dedication it would take to reach it. They knew it would be a marathon and a journey —certainly not a sprint. That led them to becoming the first climbers to reach the summit of Mount

Everest. That also led them to be named by Time Magazine as two of the 100 most influential people of the 20th century. Though the odds were stacked against me, I had no choice but to remain laser-focused. Supporters surrounded me, and my dreams for a better future for myself and the community was all the Redbull I needed.

With nothing in my checking or savings account, I purchased suits on credit. When I met with business professionals, I wanted to make sure they took me seriously. Everything I did and bought was intentional. The people I met were an investment in my future. That laser-focused mindset that I developed led me to graduate at the top of my class. That laser-focused mindset also led me to becoming one of nine other students around the world to be selected to be a part of the number one healthcare company in the world, Johnson & Johnson, Inc.

Though I had nothing to my name but a dream, I soon became the first in my family to earn a bachelor's degree. The lack of resources didn't stop me from developing a non-profit organization that empowers young students around the world to become excelling business professionals. The accusations and dirt thrown on my name did stop me from working for a Fortune 500 company making over $100,000 annually by the age of 24. What's my point? It is not about the cards you are dealt, the opportunities given, or the circumstances you are born into. It is about strategically positioning the cards in your hand, working your butt off to create opportunities, and driving your destiny by your decisions, actions, and determination. It is about embracing your failures, being the hardest worker, and keeping a positive attitude.

THE MISSION PLAN: THE DISCOVERY

Three Steps to Walking in Purpose

One of the founding fathers of the United States, Benjamin Franklin, quoted, "either write something worth reading or do something worth writing about." I love this quote because like Mr. Franklin, in my life I wanted to accomplish both. Earlier this week I was having a conversation with a good friend of mine and she was explaining everything that she wanted to accomplish in her life and even why she wanted to do it with so much passion. It's like I felt her energy on the phone and I was instantly a part of her dream of impacting millions of women through her empowering talk show. It was truly amazing to feel the transfer of energy in such a positive format, and I was so engaged with her passion and focus on accomplishing this dream. It wasn't until the emotion and passion came down that we could think with our logic instead of being so engrossed in our current emotions. Every one has a dream, everyone has all of these things that I wish for, hope for, and would love to have one day. But everyone doesn't have the how-to-guide on acquiring it. I used to be in this same predicament, all of these "what's," but not one "how." In my experience, there are three steps that I was taught in order to put the pieces together in turning that future dream into your one-day present reality.

Step One: Write It Down

I believe the best form of memorization is to write it down. I remember getting in trouble in grade school and my teachers requiring me to write down the alphabet, numbers and even sentences over and over again until my hands felt numb. I call it intellectual punishment; I hated doing it, however, it served a purpose. I believe the best form of pushing our dreams to the forefront of our priorities is by doing this same exercise and continuing to write them down consistently. Your dreams are only your dreams until you write them down. The biggest lie that I used to tell myself growing up is that I do not need to write it down, I can remember it. Until a good friend of mine, David Shands, author of Dreams Are Built Over Night, told me to never trust my memory and to write everything down. Writing down your dreams is the first step in eliminating worry and mapping out the directions towards your destination.

Step Two: Research! Research! Research!

Once you have written down that dream you have gone from the dream phase to planting the seeds of strategy towards your success. The next step in the dream manifestation process is nurturing your dream by fertilizing it with quality research. The purpose of research is to find what everyone else has seen and create a way of thinking that nobody has yet to think of. The important thing is to never stop questioning everything and let the drug of curiosity keep you high on the possibilities and not the problems. Intellectual curiosity serves as the root of the tree of your legacy and serves as the stronghold towards your individual success. Remain curious, never stop questioning and research the ins and outs of what you are trying to accomplish in your life.

Step Three: Get A Mentor

I contribute my success to my hard work, but I have had great mentorship, coaches and people that have helped me along the way on this journey. I am so appreciative to have been connected, introduced and positively influenced by those who were willing to invest their time, resources and energy into me. In my experience, my mentors saw more talent and ability to me than I ever saw in myself. Through the exposure to different opportunities, perspectives or intellectual viewpoints it helped prepare me not just be a scholar but prepared me for life itself. Through the exposure to even other great people, mentors through my life were there to let me pick their brains, listen to my frustrations and help shape my failures and mistakes into monuments of success. Through times where I may have been led astray because of distractions, they gave me direction towards my destiny.

For this challenge, you will need your notebook or journal. Answer the following questions.

1. What global issues are you passionate about solving?
2. Are their opportunities for you to travel abroad?
3. Where would you like to visit, and why?
4. What is your plan for taking a trip abroad?

THE MISSION PLAN: THE DISCOVERY

TIPS FOR SUCCESS

Don't just think about how you can change your own life, think about how you can make a difference in the lives of others.

Get involved in opportunities to learn solutions for the problems you are passionate about solving in the world.

Remember to always take time to assess after every bad mistake! Within every bad decision lies an opportunity to improve.

CHAPTER ONE
MISSION PLANNING

July 20, 1969, marked in a day in history that the world will forever remember. On this day, Apollo 11 became the first spaceflight to land two human beings on the moon successfully. Mission commander Neil Armstrong and pilot Buzz Aldrin, both American, landed the lunar module Eagle on July 20, 1969, at 20:18 UTC. Years later, we still honor the astronauts who defied history. We always talk about Apollo 11, the spaceflight that made the land. We even talk about the engineers who led the mission. What we don't acknowledge, however, are the days, years, decades, and centuries it took for the world to land its first man on the moon. The process it takes to efficiently plan a mission is very critical to its execution, outcome, and ultimately, success.

In the military, mission planning requires more than just throwing the dice and hoping for good luck. It is more critical than just booking your trip, getting there, and figuring it out as you go along. Mission planning is an art that requires an in-depth understanding of all the elements and critical factors that may negatively or positively impact the mission.

In the military, a failed mission could result in losing the lives of innocent men and women. The assessment thread of analysis is of high importance because it examines how certain threats can be negated, overcome, or exploited to give the soldiers the advantages required to execute a successful mission with zero causalities. This overall process could take days, weeks, months, and at times, even years to plan depending on the value level of the target being apprehended. The overall planning process is a vital component for success, and although luck can play a role, it is the ultimate plan, explained to the private military company (PMC) in detail that will determine the success of any mission. Before the mission is set into motion, the role of gathering on-going real-time intelligence plays a crucial role in the development of the strategic and tactical operational concepts and allows adjustments to be made to the concepts. Customarily, based upon the information gathered from intelligence, a mission profile is formed. It details the amount of ammunition, weapons, manpower, and even tactics to be followed during the mission. It is important that we understand that there is no number of weapons, ammunition, or manpower suitable for a poorly planned mission.

In business, the stakes aren't as high. Though we won't cause the death of innocent people, jobs can be lost, stock value may decrease, and the company's resources could be depleted if we do not execute projects aligned with the company's mission statement. Many companies have gone bankrupt and failed due to poor planning, which ultimately leads to poorly performing. The overall or high-level mission in business is to be profitable, innovative, competitive, and to survive. The importance of the mission statement in business creates an environment that serves as the beating heart for the organization, the lifeline, or the doctrine in which employees are hired, business is run, and the company's corporate brand is formed around.

In the military, the mission plan is assessed and memorized before the military company deploys to keep the secrecy and successful execution of the mission. In business, the mission statement is usually found on the first few pages to set the tone. The mission statement allows the reader to understand the purpose of what the business is doing. A business plan, on the other hand, is the organizational structure including titles or directors, goals, sales targets, or operational milestones in the form of a management tool to be referred to regularly. The mission statement in business is the high-value target thread assessment and gives the organization its purpose for doing what it does. Thus, making it the most vital part of any business plan.

The purpose of a mission statement is to grab your customer's attention quickly. However, it's much more than that. The mission statement is not the same as your company's slogan. It's also not the vision statement, which defines where the company is planning to go in the future and the outlook of the company. The mission statement, though included in your business plan, is not a substitute for the plan itself. However, it must be completed before you can even think to tackle the other components of the business plan. So, what is a mission statement? What does it include? It's short and concise, yet it must resonate with the employees and customers that benefit from the organization. It expresses the organization's purpose in a way that should inspire and support the ongoing commitment that the company believes to live by. Let's take American Express, a global leader in financial institution. Their mission statement says:

> "At American Express, we have a mission to be the world's most respected service brand. To do this, we have established a culture that supports our team members, so they can provide exceptional service to our customers."

Simon Sinek once quoted that customers will never love a company until their employees love it first. That same quote is repeated at Hub Spot all the time. American Express has set itself apart from any other credit card company in the world because of its missions and values. I personally would agree that they have the best customer service, and that's what they are so famous for. I love how they emphasize the need to support their employees, so their employees can support their customers. From my experience with them, they always pick up the phone within seconds, and they give follow-up calls to see if the service rendered properly and promptly. American Express has built themselves off customer service, putting the customer before their employees, and giving their employees the necessary support in helping to support the means of their customer. Simon Sinek, the author of Start with Why and many other books on professional and personal development, always quotes that everything in business trickles down from leadership to the employees.

MISSION PLANNING

The students I mentor often ask me, "Kyle, how do we create a business plan? How can we become successful business owners? How did you know how to set up your business? How did you find your purpose?" I always admonish them to start with Why. I ask them questions like,

Why do you want to be this business man?
Why do you want to sell this product?
Who is this product helping?
What is this company going to stand for?
Where are we going to be serving?
How are we going to be serving our customer?

Questions like these lead to the development of your company's mission statement, values, and the characteristics your company will live by. At IKEA, they dream big! Their mission statement could have been a promise for beautiful, affordable furniture. But, they decided that their mission statement is to make everyday life better for their customers, it's a partnership. IKEA finds deals all over the world and buys in bulk. Then they choose the furniture and pick it up at a self-service warehouse. They improve everyday life for people through furniture, at the most affordable and price-conscious price they can deliver.

Let's look at another company, Nestle. Many of you may know them for their water, hot chocolate, tea, or one of their many other brands. Nestle's mission statement is:

> "Become the world's leading nutrition health and wellness company. Our mission of good food, good life is to provide customer and consumers with the

best tasting, most nutrition choices and a wide range of food and beverage categories in eating occasions from morning to night."

Now, I always wondered to myself how Nestle went from a water company to a chocolate company, to a tea company, to a hot chocolate company. While Nestle's mission has never changed, their products are always different.

Now in life, it's the same thing. What I see when I look at you, or what you see when you look at that yourself will naturally change as you mature. Your hair may gray, your eyes lids may darken, and your skin may become less firm. When I look at you, I see a company that may go through rebranding, moves its headquarter office, undergo a few layoffs, and even makes changes in its organizational structure. However, I do not see a change in its mission statement, values, identity.

In this chapter, we will focus on scrapping your business plan and redesigning and rebranding your mission plan. What is your mission for your life? What is it that brings you joy and happiness? How do you even determine that mission? Maya Angelo stated, "My mission in life is not only survive, but to fly a do so with some compassion, some humor and some style."

It wasn't until I graduated college, had my first son, got my first job with a fortune 500 company that I was challenged on my mission statement. Through college we are always taught to get a good major to get a good job; get a good job to get a great salary; get a great salary so you can live a great lifestyle; live a great lifestyle so you can show your kids a lifestyle your parents didn't have. So, I focused on that,

MISSION PLANNING

and I accomplished that. I picked a great major and obtained a bachelor degree in finance, and worked with the number 30 company on the fortune 500 list, Johnson and Johnson. I got a great salary coming out of college, making $65,000 a year. My first bonus jumped me up to about $80,000. I never thought about morals, values, and life. They never taught us about that in class. I learned the hard way that in life, we are given instruction, and if we do not follow those instructions, our life will be chaotic. However, when we follow those instructions, we can receive blessings, gifts, awards, acknowledgments, accomplishments, and more. Early in my career, my ambition and the lack of knowledge of my mission lead to my demise.

Three months into my career at Johnson and Johnson, I thought it would be okay to spend $8,000 on a corporate card for personal expenses. Though I had a plan to pay the money back, I missed the entire principle of my actions. I had an opportunity to work with a major company, making more than many of my cohorts. Instead of being grateful and a better steward of the money I made, I was greedy. I put my need for more above the needs of the company. My actions led to me being cast out and put on suspension with the company. Without the salary, I could no longer live the life I'd grown accustomed to. Ultimately, I positioned myself to no longer be able to provide for my child. I learned a very valuable lesson. Without mission, your life is at risk for destruction – at the hand of you. I knew at this point that I needed more than just a mission statement for my business. I needed a new and improved mission statement for my life.

IT'S JUST A NAME

Many founders of companies have noted that the process of picking an organization name, logo, and motto is one of the hardest decisions to make in the early stages of the business. I experienced this first-hand as an employee of Johnson & Johnson. The process of selecting a name for a new pharmaceutical drug was very strenuous. The company had to go through many hoops and loops and tap a bunch of bells and whistles just to figure out the name of this product, and rightfully so. Companies desire to make sure that the name is not just marketable, but that it will also last. If possible, the name of the company and its products should embody the values and the distinguishing characteristic of the company or organization.

When we brainstormed the name for Project Shine, now known as the Shine Institute, it was tough. At first, we wanted to be known as Project Impact. Then, we wanted to use an acronym. Acronyms seemed to be the way to go. The more we thought about it, the more we realized that most bigger companies aren't even known for the meaning behind their initials or acronym. Here are a few companies I bet you know, but were never knowledgeable of what their acronyms/initials stood for:

>**UPS** United Parcel Service
>**AT&T** American Telephone & Telegraph
>**ADT** the alarm company American District Telegraph
>**M&M's** Mars & Murrie's
>**3M** the tape and office supply people Minnesota Mining and Manufacturing

BMW Bayerische Motoren Werke/ Bavarian Motor Works
CVS Consumer Value Stores

Though we may have never known what their initials stood for, we knew each of these companies in some shape or fashion. To us, their initials may represent just a name, but to the company, the name means so much more. It is the brand that they embody. It's the brand they stand behind. Selecting a name for your company can sometimes be difficult. The name selecting process is about more than utilizing those linguistics tricks we learned in business schools. It's about selecting something that will carry you for years and years to come. It's about selecting a name that will become a household name. Sometimes, as a small business, your likely to be a little bolder about your name.

Yes, sometimes companies rename themselves, as part of a rebranding effort. This can sometimes be the consequence of a major screw up, a scandal, or the merging of companies.

I remember when Cingular Wireless merged with and became AT&T. If you think hard enough, I'm sure you can recall dozens of companies who have changed their name or have branded themselves with other companies over the years. In addition to rebranding and merging, sometimes, name changes happen simply because the company's initial name wasn't memorable. They didn't have the strength to take the company to the next level.

So, don't be afraid to rebrand yourself. I get it; life is a little bit different than changing your name. We're given a name from the day we are born, and it is our responsibility to

THE MISSION PLAN: THE DISCOVERY

live up to it. While it may be hard to get people to change how they address you, you decide what you answer to. Challenge yourself to live beyond your past and be the person you desire to be!

When we found out we were having a son, my child's mother and I went back and forth for months to figure out a name. We played all these different name games and even went down the alphabet list, calling every name that came to mind. A- Adam? Andrew? Anthony? No? B- Blake? Byron? Bobby? No? C- Charles? Carl? No? We would read baby books, google impactful names, and dozens of other strategies until one day, we decided on Carter. Even though he was born with this name, he didn't begin to respond to it until much later. It's not that he couldn't hear us calling him Carter, it's just that it took him some time to realize that it was his name and that is what he had to answer to. We couldn't stop calling him Carter because he couldn't recognize it was his name yet. We had to keep calling him by his name until he realized we were speaking to him! Your business and life are the same way. What you learn to answer to is who you will become.

When a phone malfunctions or has a low success rate, it's not the phone that catches the backlash. Instead, the phone's manufacturer catches it. People barely remember the horrible phone, but they will always remember that the company released a faulty device. Instead of acknowledging that there may have been a simple mistake in the product or device, people assume that something is wrong with the entire company. Your life is quite similar. If we make a mistake, people don't talk about the error; they talk about the characteristics, the morals, and the values of that person. They talk about the character (or the lack thereof) of that person. Every action we make, every deed we do, every approach we take, and everything we say, is what we are remembered for. Denzel Washington once said, "You never seen a U-Haul following behind a hearse. I know that's an old quote, but what he explained was that it's not about what we have in life, it's about what we do with what we have. We cannot take anything we have with us to the grave. The Egyptians tried to do it for years. They believed that you had to pay a token to get into the afterlife, and if you are buried with your riches, you would be able to take them into the afterlife with you. Years and centuries later, they have been robbed of the wealth, riches, and treasures they collected. Again, it's not about what we have, but what we do with what we have. It's not about Apple becoming the number one technology company in the world; it is about them creating a new wave of technology that is accessible to everyone in the world.

It is not about 28-year-old Mark Zuckerberg creating Facebook and making it a multi-billion corporation, but it is about the good deeds that he has done to provide the world with a service and be able to redevelop third world economies through his plans to create a corporate communicative world against tyranny. It is not about the efforts of BMW to create cutting edge technology within their vehicles, but it's about them creating these models of renewable energy to be able to save the earth and creating jobs for people. All companies in life have a social responsibility, a corporate responsibility to be able to give back to those who have bought their products or used their products through jobs or just systems and products that make life better. In life, our character responsibility and our cultural responsibility is to give back to those who will come after us. The power and the purpose of this chapter are to understand the power of our name and that we are all more than just our social security numbers, employee ID numbers, student numbers, or driver license numbers. Our name is our legacy, and everything we do in life will echo into eternity.

Be morally correct and let your values lead your life. It's not about what you have; it's about who you help. Whether you're running a fortune 500 company or you're still a student, it is your responsibility to be the change you wish to see in the world. It is your corporate responsibility as a business owner to give back, but it is also your responsibility to give back to those who did not have the same opportunities as you. Because what we do in life echoes into eternity, the first step is to find a name, but the second step is to solidify the mission after we realize the power of the name that we selected.

As we discussed in book one, before an employee can get hired to be the CEO of a company, they should first realize how to become the CEO of themselves. Too many times in life, we draw lines between our personal and professional lifestyle, creating a sense of falsehoods instead of empowering authenticity. When this is done, it creates a lack of effort on the job and a lack of loyalty to the company. The mission statement of a business is critical and serves as the lifeline of a business. We must first understand the importance of having a mission statement in our lives before we value the importance of the mission statement elsewhere. The importance of the mission statement or our vision statement in life sets the tone for our lives, gives us a sense of purpose, encourages us to set and meet goals, and drives us to work towards our dreams. Our personal mission statements create a reason for getting up earlier than usual to finish a task, the strength to finish that paper late at night so you can graduate on time, or even trying out again for the dance team even though you didn't make the final cut the year before.

If someone was to type your name into a search engine what would be the description that comes up describing you? Would this description align with what you want the world to describe you as, or is there so much more? Do your mistakes motivate you or have they created the fear to not continue to work for what keeps you up at night? Before we can find a solution to a problem, we must bring awareness to the external symptoms of the problem so we can develop an internal solution. So, what truly is your mission, your purpose, or your vision for the life that you are currently living or even the life that you dream to live one day? Practices may change during our lives, but the principles should never be altered. By developing a personal mission statement, you instantly define the principles in your life that you are going to live by to align with your passion. Is your mission to lead or to inspire? Is your mission to love or to empower? Your mission statement could be as short as 3 words or as long as 30 words. As long as you understand your purpose you will begin to build strategies around your priorities. So, before we move into the meat of this magical madness, I'd like to pose the first questions.

For this challenge and the following challenges, you'll need a notebook or your journal.

1. What is your mission statement?
2. What do you stand for?
3. How do you determine your character?
4. How are you benefiting the world?

TIPS FOR SUCCESS

Make a mission statement for your life before you focus on making a mission statement for your business.

Define your mission and goals in life. Have an, "Everyone can win!" attitude.

Research the mission statements of other businesses, especially those in your market.

"At first, they will ask why you're doing it. Later, they'll as how you did it."

– Anonymous

CHAPTER TWO
SHARPENING SUCCESS SKILLS

What is your definition of success? Do you think success is predicated in school by test scores, GPA, grades, student performance, confidence, or development? Do you think success in business or life is predicated on the amount of money and power you have? Or, is it predicated on something else? According to our society, it is about how high you are within a company or an organization, how much money you have in your bank account, or how many people you are connected to in your social and business network. We asked 100 CEOs to give us their definition of success, and the ranges in the results were staggering. Can the dictionary really define success for us? Or, is this something that each person must define for themselves? What is the success spectrum? Is it different for each person? One thing I have realized over this journey is that whether your definition of success has money involved, luxury cars or homes, helping people, or building a billion-dollar technology empire, success for everyone must include being happy and fulfilled.

When I realized that I began to miss the special moments of life focusing on what I thought was success, I began to make the necessary changes in my personal and professional life. I was so busy focusing on future fortune that I forgot to appreciate the present process. I realized that I couldn't be so focused on what I wanted without first appreciating and being grateful for the current position I was in and what I had. Looking back on teaching from mentors, they would always tell me to be humble and remind me how important family, people, and legacy was because what you believe and what people think of you when they hear your name are the two things that could never be taken away.

I truly believe that success is a self-discovery. The first point of success is being a go-getter, a self-starter. That ambition drives the action behind your ideas. You can't teach someone how to be a go-getter, how to be ambitious, or how to be a self-starter. You can't assign it to someone and they just get it. I truly believe that by, empowering people over a period of time, acknowledging their efforts, and guiding them through accomplishing those small goals will build the confidence within them to accomplish the bigger tasks. They must find the passion within them. Successful people engage differently, approach life differently, and they ask different questions. Once they begin to ask those different questions, they get different answers that truly change their perspective on life. It is the small things that build the belief, once you have the belief, you instill confidence. Once you are confident, you can truly accomplish anything. Because you then have a skill called resilience. You won't quit, you believe in yourself and you are willing to give up all the alternatives to truly follow your dreams and make them a reality. That is what success looks like. You must acknowledge success before you obtain success.

So many people have asked me, Kyle, "How are you so confident? Have you always been this way? Where does it come from?" I always answer, "I believed in myself." Though it sounds so easy to do, there are specific steps that I have taken to get to where I am today. I am at the point today where whatever I see, feel, and touch is an opportunity to make it the best it can possibly be. Instead of looking at life as an obligation, I look at everything in life as an opportunity. I want you to take the time at the beginning of each week to write out your goals. Write your weekly to-do list, write your weekly goals, and under that on the same page, write your monthly, yearly, and long-term aspirations or dreams.

Each week as you set goals, look at them as small tasks even though You are working towards your dream. You plant little seeds of confidence inside your mind and body every time you cross something off that list. You are building confidence and belief in yourself to do something differently, to do more than what is expected, and to be better than you were the month, week, or even year before. You must understand that it is those small increments that truly lead your life to long-term change. It starts WITH YOU! Just think back when you were younger and how you felt when your parents asked you if you were finished with your homework, and you had already had done it at school. You had time to play with your friends! Think back on that time when your teacher reminded you in class about your project due Friday, and you finished it early so you could just make the final changes the day before and freshen up. Or, even remember if you had a weekly or daily to-do list and you accomplished everything by the end of the day, do you remember that feeling? Yes, it was a great feeling. You felt productive, accomplished, CONFIDENT. Confidence, just like success, is a process. After taking small steps every day, eventually, you wake up one morning and think you can take on the whole world!

Confidence is not about performance and how good you are at something; it is about the passion that you have for what you do. When you have that passion, you create an innate ability to accomplish whatever the steps are that align with that passion. You will work to be the best at it and remain resilient to becoming better than your competition. Look at today's music industry and how the quality of artists has declined from the days of Prince, Michael Jackson, Marvin Gaye, Biggie Smalls, and even the Temptations. Today, music is all about entertainment, and a lot of artists are not in it because of their heart; they are in it because it provides an opportunity to leverage a skill into capital. When you are leveraging, you are trying to gain a benefit, material, or some monetary award. When you have a true passion, you will do it for nothing; you are not looking for the next paycheck, you are not worried about competition, you are just focused on your love for whatever it may be. If you are a graphic artist, you are not drawing to be put in a museum; you are drawing to release those emotions, to paint a story, or to develop the masterpiece in your mind. When you are passionate about a sport, it is not about the check; it's about the opportunity just to continue to play no matter the weather or the compensation. Looking at today's world, people are so focused on profit that they forget ever to find and live within their passion. This results in mediocrity, complacency, and being downright average. When you are just good at something, that is all that it merely is. A talent. Talent only gets you so far, but when you align work-ethic with what you truly love you become successful.

That feeling of always wanting money, wealth and just more used to drive me to the point of almost having anxiety attacks. I've met few people who genuinely wanted success as bad as I did, and I don't think I will ever meet someone with the same passion for change as I have. I was on a phone conversation with my friend one evening and telling her how bad I just wanted to be successful, how I wanted more, and how bad I just wanted to make money because I was so tired of struggling. She made a very good point and spoke to me about the importance of patience. She reminded me that it is not just about the now, it is about positioning yourself to be successful later.

It is vital to understand the importance of not being so caught up in your current circumstance where you get stuck there and never strategically build a vision plan for how to get out of that spot and create opportunities. Redirect that passion, ambition, and fire into something positive and innovative. In my case, I put it towards something entrepreneurial. I call it the idea of empowering entrepreneurial energy. You do that by transferring that want for success into strategic steps.

TRIPLE E
Empowering Entrepreneurial Energy

Empowering to give (someone or something) the power or the authority to do something
Entrepreneurial Characterized by the taking of financial risks in the hope of profit; enterprising
Energy A person's physical and mental powers, typically as applied to a task or activity.

The concept of Triple E is charging you to give power to your dreams in the belief of enterprising, by elevating your physical and mental powers by focusing on the steps aligned with how to get there. In life, the choices that we make are either an investment or an expense, so we must stop spending our time on activities that are not going to yield us a return towards our dreams. I believe that before we can acquire wealth, before we can accept payment, or before we can open a line of credit, we must manage the first currency, which is the currency of time. A wise man told me to show him how I manage my time, and he could find a correlation on how I spend my money. I always like to give this math problem to help people understand.

60 Seconds in a Minute
X
60 Minutes in an Hour
X
24 Hours in a Day = 86, 400 Seconds in a Day

Every day we get a $86,400-dollar investment every day into our life account, how are we managing our currency and helping to manage this investment? What percentage goes into our dreams daily? What percentage goes to that project you've been putting off, that book you've wanted to write, that recipe that you wanted to perfect, or even that house you wanted to buy? What percentage of that investment are you wasting on meaningless tasks or bad habits that don't yield you any return on the investment? There is a famous quote by an anonymous writer, "Time is free, but it's priceless. You can't own it, but you can use it. You can't keep it, but you can spend it. Once you've lost it, you can NEVER get it back."

Your dream isn't waiting for you to come when you are ready, when you have more time to put towards it, or when you are ready to stop being lazy and procrastinating. Every day that you wait, waste, or spend, is a day that you lose. Right now, I want you to spend time on recognizing where your time is spent. Make a daily schedule and began to plan productive activities that help to accelerate you and empower that entrepreneurial energy inside of you. Wake up a bit earlier and get that run in that you always said you were going to commit to, go back into your room and finish that book you've been telling yourself you are going to finish, and get back to that business plan and start jotting down ideas so you can begin to make them into realities. Jim Rohn quoted, "Time is more valuable than money. You can get more money, but you cannot get more time." It is time to own YOUR time and to stop letting time OWN YOU. If you are going to waste your time, waste it wisely.

Sometimes in our society, we are so focused on money, materials, wealth, the car we want to drive, the house we want to live in, or the woman or man we want. The reality of it is that the idolization of these things by the media in our society doesn't make it any better; it adds fuel to the false fire. These things in our culture signify success and wealth. If you have those things, you are granted the opportunity of having a voice amongst the people.

Wearing tailored suits makes you credible, driving a fancy vehicle makes you honorable, and living in a nice home makes you a walking success story. I truly believe the pursuit to be profitable eliminates the quality in what you are doing. If you look at the greatest innovators, writers, painters, athletes, or even politicians, the one thing they have in common is not their work ethic or skills. The one thing these people have in common is the passion and love for what they are doing and that is what helped them to accelerate in their perspective areas. It wasn't about the money, it wasn't about the status, it wasn't about the signing bonuses or contracts. It was about the true nature of what they were doing and the craft in which they were pursuing. This pursuit of happiness and fulfillment brought out creativity, quality, and even greatness amongst these different legends. The passion for this craft wasn't formed by the profit that could potentially come and that is what accelerated them into being the best in every facet. When we look at the Michelangelo's, Da Vinci's, Einstein's, Jordan's, Job's, or even Greek philosophers, they all studied their craft, practiced, and learned their craft, and proceeded into perfecting their craft in a way not built off the paparazzi, but off pure passion. The tasks weren't an activity, they were a lifestyle, a livelihood.

You must love what you do, study what you want, and be an expert in your profession. Einstein continued to study his inventions, Steve Jobs wanted to revolutionize technology, Jay-Z had a love for music and being the best hip-hop artist of the 20th century, and Barack Obama just wanted to bring change. Even after they tasted success, they kept pushing, learning, and growing. This allowed them to achieve even more success.

Some of the most significant and celebrated politicians, authors, painters, or artists weren't focused on the profit that was to come by their gift; it was a passion and love for what they did that ended up bringing the highest form of quality. I'll use living at home as an example. Every day, you continue to get bills on top of bills on top of bills. Let's say your phone bill is $450, Wi-Fi and television bill is $200, car note is $300, and you have other bills you haven't even counted. What do you think life would be like if you invested all that money into your passion, into your dreams, and started to position your finances and resources into where you are trying to go? A lot of times, people say that their passion doesn't really have a way to become profitable. But most of the world's most wealthy people had that same thought and got people to believe in whatever they were selling to the point where it brought in that first customer, first $1,000 profit, first $100,000 income and now is worth billions in assets. Those passions turned into ideas, those ideas turned into plans, those plans turned into strategies, those strategies were executed, and then it successfully turned into profit. All this from just believing in yourself? You bet.

That same investment could be the same investment that you put into your career and dreams. The amount of time binge-watching television shows, scrolling on social media, searching videos on YouTube or even going out and spending time with your friends could be the same amount of time you spend working towards living within your purpose. Time is the first currency you must invest in life. Where you spend your time will determine the course of You, Incorporated every day. Every time you spend time on other things other than yourself and your passion, you take money away from the company. What are you doing to pour or to invest in yourself and your dreams? The greatest investment in life is the investment we make into ourselves. It isn't in that company, that stock, that bond, or that real estate company; the best investment is in our destiny. It is the one stock that will always increase in value and is the one bond that has no residual. It is that one real estate investment that will continue to build equity regardless of the market, location or economy. Every day, we continue to watch the stock market go up and down and spend our money on companies, clothes, materials, gas, and other products that may be led by a want or need. You must be an investor and stop spending all your assets on materials that don't yield you a return on your investment.

Jim Rohn, known as America's Foremost Business Philosopher, stated, "A formal education will make you a living but self-education will make you a fortune." So many times in my life, I was broke, going through financial struggles, absent of resources, and just in a place where I couldn't provide for myself and be self-sufficient. Because of my upbringing, growing up in a two-parent middle-class family, a lot of people looked at me as having whatever I needed and wanted because I wore nice clothes, drove nice cars, and lived in a nice 5-bedroom house in the suburbs of

Lawrenceville, Georgia. But what people didn't know was all the struggles that I faced and the battles that were being thrown at me every day.

The clothes I wore were purchased on credit, the cars I drove were leased because of my mother's company, and the house we lived in was financed, and I never had to pay any bills, rent, or contribute anything because my parents took care of it all. With all the odds in my favor, I still managed to find myself up to my neck in $20,000 of personal debt, late on student loan payments, without a job, and without a car, because I racked up too many speeding tickets. Because of my excessive stability, it cast a net around me that led to my lack of self-sufficiency. I was fortunate and grateful enough to have the resources, but I was young, immature, and uneducated enough to make the wrong decisions that led to the wrong choices that led to the position and state in which I was in. It is not about the resources; it is about the choices that we make. It is what we decide when we are faced with options and finding ways to create opportunities and not an excuse for failure. It was a choice for me to follow society's view on success by going to college, keeping my grades high, and graduating with honors.

Instead of just going to college, I didn't want to be like the 79% of people that read books during a given year or even the 27% of people that didn't pick up a book. I wanted to be like the 1-2% by reading multiple books throughout a given year. My curiosity and interest in knowledge and success began to become my focus; it became my hobby and day job. Book clubs were formed, and we started to read one book a month to one every two weeks to completing a

THE MISSION PLAN: THE DISCOVERY

52-week book challenge and reading a book a week during a year. It wasn't just focusing on formal education, exams, midterms, pop-quizzes, and book knowledge in school; I wanted to be a student of my passion and use all the knowledge out there to pave a way to getting there. Instead of going out every weekend, I chose to go out and get mentors. Instead of indulging in social media and gossip, I began to fill my mind with lectures and started to listen to audiobooks and podcast of entrepreneurs and public speakers. Instead of being the life of the party, I became the person who would speak life into people.

In a society that will never be problem proof, it is natural to focus on problems. The reality of it is that when you focus on problems, more problems are created, more problems are brought to you, and more issues begin to arise. Instead, we must focus on creating solutions for the problems we see. Then, opportunities will yield to us, and the world will begin to align with what we want instead of what we are going through. Learning to think differently, act differently, and live differently is a skill that the successful have mastered and perfected. It is not about focusing on the everyday minute; it is about focusing on the possibilities of change, opportunity, and innovation. Life is a rollercoaster; it has its up and downs. Just because we drop in stock, speed, or acceleration doesn't mean that the ride is over. It doesn't mean that your dreams or the work is over. It means that something better, faster, and bigger is getting ready take place in your life. Rollercoasters at amusement parks are so much fun, but the real question is, is the work you are doing, the state of your life, your current position fun? Are you having fun with the daily tasks? Are you filled with tasks or creating and providing opportunities? Are you working on someone's else projects or are you projecting your success and profit in the future? We must have fun with our lives and not be so blinded by the lens of reality and create our reality based upon what we want to see, what we want to have, what we want to earn, and what we want to become. Don't focus on the hardships of today, begin to focus on the opportunities that could be provided for tomorrow.

MEETING WITH THE MOGUL

When I was 17 years old, I had the opportunity to travel to Winston Salem, North Carolina and meet with one of the most successful, hard-working, innovative businessman I have ever met. This man had managed to own multiple car dealerships and not only did he own them, but they were also consistently the top performing dealerships for decades. I didn't know what to expect when I met him. I wasn't sure if he was going to be arrogant or someone who was humble. I had so many questions prepared for him, and my goal was just to learn how he did it. I wanted to learn how he created such wealth from humble beginnings. I remember sitting in the waiting area, waiting for his arrival into the audience, and watching how his employees greeted each customer. I noticed how well business was being conducted and how there was such a sense of pride and comradery amongst his staff. I remember getting there about 15-20 minutes early so I could be prompt and prepared for the day ahead. Through the short time where I sat in my chair, I was never alone, and I was offered water, coffee, test drives of the vehicles, information about the vehicles, and even snacks. It was hands-down the best customer service I had ever witnessed and experienced. It set such a great impression for the dealership. Our appointment was set for 10:30 AM, and at 10:25 AM, he walked in the office with his tailored suit, no tie, and suit jacket. I remember watching him speak to every single person on the sales floor and shook their hand. He spoke to all the customers individually and asked them how their day was going. He proceeded to me, shook my hand, smiled and welcomed me into his office. Through our conversation, I developed seven personal opinions of his character as a man and as the owner of the business. He was relentless, self-motivated, fair, sharp, and a loving family man that treated his staff not as employees but as a family. Through our hours of being together, there were five points that I wanted to be able to highlight for this topic. Great managers and successful businesses have fundamental principles and values that generate expectations from employees and create a company's competitive advantage.

The Power of Principles:

Question: What are your principles?

Mogul's Remarks: You never have to tell someone a lie to sell a product. If you tell someone you're going to do something, you do it. Your word is your bond. I can't stand a liar and a thief. Integrity, professionalism, excellence is what I value and the environment I work to create. I will not let a client disrespect my employees. I will go to war for my employees, and no sale is worth diminishing the values or character of what took so long to build. I trust my people with decisions until they give me a reason not to. That is the importance of training your employees, if they fail, I have failed.

Excessive Expectations:

Question: What do you expect out of your employees?

Mogul's Remarks: I expect them to take ownership and hold themselves accountable for their actions, decisions, and performance. I ask them, if this was your business how would you handle this situation. If you were the owner of this store, what would you do uniquely different? Then I would tell them to do it. You have to empower people to make decisions that would bring value to the organization. That is the cost of doing business, empowering people, and investing in your team. I give my people the benefit of the doubt; they are people too so you must treat people as such.

Creating Competitive Advantages:

Question: What is the company's competitive advantage?

Mogul's Remarks: We put family first. All the amenities, services and programs are created specifically for our customers. We want our customers to feel as if they do not buy a car from us they are doing themselves an injustice. It is much bigger than the car sale; it is the relationships. I create a value proposition, and we stick to them. Price is what you pay; value is what you get. The thing you have least of is time. Time is invaluable, so you must maximize your time by creating value for your customers. If I can save customers time, then what is that worth to them to purchase a vehicle from us? The true value of their time is priceless.

THE MISSION PLAN: THE DISCOVERY

Put YOUR Business First:

Question: How close are you in your business?

Mogul's Remarks: I know everything about this business from services, parts, and sales. I know about each deal being made every day, and I am in the business, not just running it. I don't play games; I gets busy. I know every detail of this business, not just the financial statements, I am involved with my people and ask them when I can help them. A team is only as strong as its leader. If I have to wash cars, take out the trash, or take a customer for a test drive, I do so. I am no more important than the newest person here. I am a part of the team as well.

Regulating Routines:

Question: What is your daily plan?

Mogul's Remarks: Routines are critical to business success. You have to stick to a routine, if things go bad, you can pinpoint what was different and what changed. I come in every day and speak to everyone in the building. I then go directly to my office and call each person in my office and check on the business, see what is going on, where we are at with any deals, and what the daily goals and plans may be for that given day. From the body shop, detailing, service, and sales floor, I know every single detail of this business. After I meet with the team, it is time to get to work and start making it happen.

Mogul Motivation

Question: What other advice would you give to up and coming businessmen and women?

Mogul's Remarks: Business is all about perception and doing what you have to do to keep your clients business and keep your clients happy. Customer service and being able to provide quality products quickly will keep your customers happy and returning for more. The worst thing in business is to lose business. The overall business is key in owning, operating, and successfully running a business. Here, we don't believe in such a thing as a "bad deal." The only thing is being able to write the deal, work the deal, and take the deal so we can assure that our customers are happy and taken care of. Another thing that is important is product management and effectively managing your inventory. If you don't have it, you can't sell it. Your product inventory has to fit the customer's need. The business is not about keeping the products stocked that cost the least, that you may like the best, or maybe that makes you the most money when they are sold. You have to continue to put your customers first. It takes more of you, to run a successful business.

When you master the art of duplicating yourself, you will make people want to emulate what you do. This begins with leading by example and providing value for your staff by always learning new things and staying ahead of the game. You want to be able to have the best processes, train people, lead people, and find people to run these processes effectively. You can't do everything by yourself, and a good leader develops great leaders. Lastly, you must understand that the only thing you have going for you is you. Don't point fingers and do nothing. It is up to you, and it starts with you every day in the mirror. You are the one that is going to make a change and truly make a difference.

The Mogul's Mastery
Question: What skills do you believe are important in owning a business?

Mogul's Remarks: The first advice is to be articulate with your speech and pronounce the words the way they are spelled. You do not want people to judge you based upon your articulation of speech. One of the things that I was taught at a young age was the importance of getting rid of all the objections. When people talk about price, immediately go to value and create that value proposition for them to understand that this purchase is more than a product and that it aligns with their purpose. I believe a lot of students lack the fundamental skills to be successful not just in business, but in life. Here are a few that I wrote for your visit today that I believe would help you grow into a successful businessman.

Important Skills to Master
- Effective Communication
- Leadership Qualities and Characteristics
- Influencing and Motivating
- Interpersonal and Personal Branding
- Professionalism in Business

Answer the following questions honestly.

1. What are your principles?
2. What do you expect from your employees?
3. What is your company's advantage?
4. How close do you plan to be to your business?
5. What is your daily plan for your business?

TIPS FOR SUCCESS

Success is not predicated in school by test scores, GPA, grades, student performance, confidence, or development?

In life, the choices that we make are either an investment or an expense, so we must stop spending our time on activities that are not going to yield us a return towards our dreams.

The best investment you can ever make is the investment in your destiny!

CHAPTER THREE

TEAMWORK IS WHY THE DREAM WORKS

James Cash Penny quoted, "The five separate fingers are five independent units. Close them, and the fist multiplies strength. This is organization." When an organization has unified power, it leads to unilateral organizational success where all employees, staffers, or team players benefit individually. Organizational success, no matter how well the facilities, how quality the products, and how efficiently marketed, are only as good as its people and those who operate the business. Stephen Covey quoted, "An empowered organization is one in which individuals have the knowledge, skill, desire and opportunity to personally succeed in a way that leads to collective organizational success." I was fortunate enough to learn this early as an entrepreneur instead of when it was too late and had to lead to offices closing, employees getting laid off, and people not being able to take care of their families. There was a time in my career where I almost gave it all up and threw in the towel. When I received a text from

THE MISSION PLAN: THE DISCOVERY

my assistant at 6:30 AM in the morning on March 23, 2017, it brought me to a realization that things needed to change and that I was putting myself before the business. The text stated:

> "I have an assignment for you. Provide me with three good reasons as to why I should continue working for project shine. A caveat: At this point, leadership experience and the philanthropic angle are too shallow an answer. I have a hundred different ways that I could fulfill both without expending an extra thought to shine. Think about it and provide me an answer by the end of today, preferably via email."

A mentor of mine always describes teamwork as being, "the most critical point in organization success." The most important part about any business, community initiative, or sports team is the team. In short, a team is having people with similar visions working towards the same goals, putting in similar efforts by leveraging each other's strengths to counter any weaknesses. Organizational failure doesn't happen overnight, it is a timeline of small miscommunications, misunderstandings, missing of deadlines or bad business decisions over a period of time that lead to an overall organization declining in value. I now had a realization that everything that I envisioned, dreamed up, and even pictured in my head wasn't going to happen at the time I wanted it to happen.

Everything that I worked for and believed in and even all of the resources, money spent, time taken up, was for nothing because I wasn't going to be successful. Business isn't about struggling, success in business comes from resiliency and rebounding. I didn't look at this time as a loss, I looked at this time, yet again, as another learning opportunity to understand I wasn't executing and leading effectively. It is not about the resources thrown into a project, it isn't about the sophisticated PowerPoint decks, great website, or even the great marketing campaign with videos and amazing photos. Business is about quality products, quality people, and effective performance.

Sometimes when we are faced with a crossroad decision, we have to reroute, go off road and create a new way of getting to our destination. Sometimes we have to go against the grain, change the approach, and produce creative solutions to internal problems. It wasn't about throwing more resources at the problems, letting go of employees, or rebranding the organizational name; some mistakes are yet formed to be monuments of success. Originally, I formed Project SHINE as a non-profit organization but because of the business structure I was constrained to certain rules and regulations and, at times, I couldn't be as flexible as I needed to be.

In this structure, even if you are the founder, your ideas then have to go through a board of directors to agree upon before actions can be taken. There was a certain financial structure that prevented us from making quick investments in the marketplace and rolling out major programs for our students. It provided us with the greatest opportunity to serve, however, lacked a path to sustainability and scalability. Business is about breaking through obstacles and letting them not block the path, but be the path towards our ultimate goals, dreams, and destinies. The true message here is that no matter how much you love your brand, there is going to come a time when you have to change things up. The markets may shift, the economy may create new competitive forces preventing you from operating in certain spaces, or even new challenges may arise that creates different opportunities for growth. In the article "5 Examples of Rebranding Done Right," Jayson DeMers explains stories of major corporations that leveraged rebranding to bring heightened success. He writes about the story of Burberry, the British Luxury Fashion brand housed and headquartered in London, England. Its main fashion hours focuses on and distributes Trench coats, ready-to-wear outwear, fashion accessories, fragrances, sunglasses, and even cosmetics.

Burberry is a fantastic example of how a brand can change its image with a few simple marketing tweaks. Just a couple decades ago, Burberry was suffering from a bad reputation, being associated with gang wear. In 2001, a new creative director, Christopher Bailey, took over and started introducing new products like swimwear and trench coats that were unaffiliated with previous images of the brand. Celebrity endorsements from Emma Watson and Kate Moss helped cement the new image of Burberry, and now the company is a major luxury brand, touted as a symbol of high class and wealth.

We are all given the same hours each day, we just use those hours differently. In business, we are given the same resources, information, and access, but it is up to us to understand how to use what we have in front of us the best way possible. Bill Richardson quoted, "We cannot accomplish all that we need to do without working together." Before you can get to the point where everyone is working effectively, it is important to get people on the same page in order to accomplish that same goal. The best way of managing success begins with managing the expectations. I learned quickly that I expected too much too soon and wasn't executing in the space that people believed I already created. The organization was over-marketing and under-producing. We were over-selling and when we had customers to buy, we lacked the product in order to deliver. Moving forward in my career, I used the mistakes early on in our organization to define the success that would come in our seven-year succession plan. We redefined our expectations, suspended current programs, and reevaluated our plan of action. We had to create a team from ground up so our company wouldn't fall to the ground. The better your team is at the foundational steps, the better success you will have in the long run. The expectations, personality traits, working styles, or any concerns should be acknowledged and discussed at the beginning so you can understand and learn what works best for the team.

Great leaders know how to take people from different backgrounds with different personality traits and working styles, and bring them together having them all work together effectively to bring organization success. When you develop a sense of comradery, different people begin to specialize in different tasks, leading to the organization, team, or business minimizing the weakness and maximizing efficiency. Don't let people misinterpret your passion with aggression. Be able to adapt and be flexible with your team.

Before we can form a process or a plan of action, we have to understand the purpose and answer the big "why." One of the major problems in leadership is the lack of communication due to ineffective listening. Listening to your team members and staff is critical in solving problems and even having organization success. Statistics show when your employees feel they have a voice and could give their opinion, it increases work efficiency. Listen to your people and work with them to simplify their workload. I read a quote once that teamwork divides the workload, but multiplies the success. The power of building of great relationships within your team is critical. When employees are invested in, nurtured, and empowered, they will go the extra mile to be successful not only for their managers but for the overall organization. When you offer your help with everything and can know every facet of the operational decisions within your business, the team looks at you as a coach or a mentor and not only as a "boss." Give your team a way to resolve, show them how to get results, and empower them to come up with innovative ideas that could potentially lead to organizational success.

People and processes are the most critical ingredient in business success. If people can't execute the processes you're wasting your time; if you are wasting time you are losing money, if you are losing money, you are going to have to be on your butt. Have a team of people that are smarter than you so it can, in the long run, elevate you to be better, make better decisions, and elevate your people.

THE KING'S KEYS
- Speak to your identity, if you do not know who you are it is hard for you to figure out where you are going.
- Investing in your future is the ultimate investment and will never come back with insufficient funds.

- You cannot settle for mediocracy; you cannot keep waiting for success to come, you must go out and work towards it and change the culture of society
- You either live in intention or die by default
- Have a philosophy of dying empty, and don't live a life of regret. Master all your gifts and experience life.
- Leverage your smaller accomplishments to build lasting confidence
- You must make decisions that line up with stable families and vibrant communities
- You must begin to delete our negative options and add focus on positive realities
- Think beyond the mainstream. Competition sharpens your skills. Your mind is more powerful than your hands. Solve problems with your intellect, not your weaponry.
- If you fail to plan you are planning to fail
- Your goal without a plan is yet a dream with a deadline
- Your vision is a future objective with the collection of various goals that can be accomplished over a period.
- With no structure and direction, your house of life is sure to collapse.

THE MISSION PLAN: THE DISCOVERY

Pull out your notebook or journal and answer the following questions.

1. What do you want to accomplish?
2. How can that bring value to the business?
3. How can that bring value to team members? How can that benefit you?

TIPS FOR SUCCESS

Organizational failure doesn't happen overnight, it is a timeline of small miscommunications, misunderstandings, missing of deadlines or bad business decisions over a period of time that lead to an overall organization declining in value.

Don't let people misinterpret your passion with aggression. Be able to adapt and be flexible with your team.

When you are faced with a crossroad decision, reroute, go off road, and create a new way of getting to your destination.

"Success is most often achieved by those who don't know that failure is inevitable."

- Coco Chanel

CHAPTER FOUR
3...2...1...JUMP!

One sunny afternoon, I enjoyed time with friends from across the United States. The temperature was close to 90 degrees. My skin peeled from the absence of sunscreen. I constantly looked at the temperature gauge in the car before finally grabbing sunscreen to rub on my neck and chest. The location was not your normal day in the middle of February. The stage was set as an underwater cave in Mexico where I stood above a pool of natural water approximately 60 feet down that housed some of the most beautiful underwater creatures I had ever seen, mixed with the natural beauty of plants and purpose. A purpose to not swim, but instead to challenge the status quo, realize a passion, and jump off the cliff! It had always been a dream of mine to go cliff diving and feel the thrill of jumping off a high cliff into a body of water where all my fears, trials, tribulations, and doubt would be washed away once I came up from being underwater. I'll never forget the feeling of complete and utter nervousness I felt as I prepared to leap. Genuine anxiety-producing stimuli flowed through my veins and stuck in my stomach as I looked down into that water. All my friends were taking the leaps, and I continued to get to the edge and then back up and say, "Maybe another time, I don't want it that bad. I don't want to fall and get hurt or anything. I am going to sit this one out." The chemical imbalances in my brain caused many unusual feelings, and I didn't know how to handle it besides distancing myself from the environment and leaving the situation. As I walked away from the cliff and back on the other side where my friends had swum, I began to feel worse, but this wasn't a feeling of nervousness. This was now a feeling of disappointment caused by the nonfulfillment of my hope or expectation to take that first jump into the pool of nirvana.

At that moment, all the times I didn't jump into my dreams played through my mind. It reminded me of those friends that had so much talent, but were nervous and fearful of what could happen if they were to tap into their full potential. It reminded me even of that time when I wanted to be a doctor, but I backed out because of my terrible experience taking biochemistry. It reminded me of the regret I felt from choosing an easy major…the easy way out if you will. What would have happened if I would have just jumped into that opportunity? What would have happened if I would have challenged myself a little bit more and worked a little bit harder? What would basketball be if Michael Jordan gave up? What would the world be if Thomas Edison or Benjamin Franklin stopped after the first failed experiment? These questions and many like them ran through my mind as my friends leaped and swam back to meet me, still standing, contemplating, and afraid. At that moment, I had a choice to walk away, but in the pit of my stomach, I knew that if I walked away, I would become comfortable with walking away in other areas of my life.

In life, we typically don't know enough about the outcome to make a confident leap. We fool ourselves and say, "When I do more research, I'll get out there!" The truth of the matter is, we won't always have all the details. However, we will never know what we don't know unless we JUMP! A lot of times in life, we are challenged by obstacles in the form of cliffs, mountains, or sometimes just diving boards. It is up to us to take the leap of faith and jump into the ocean of opportunity so we can dive deep into our accomplishments, be fearless, and have fun with our passions.

The first step to realizing how to jump is realizing that jumping starts with YOU taking the first step forward. When I realized that sunny afternoon in Mexico that it was up to me to face those fears and revolutionize those regrets, I began to redirect my steps towards the cliff yet again instead of running from fears. In those moments of nervousness, doubt, and even fear, just take a deep breath, close your eyes, and take that leap of faith into your dreams! After I took that deep breath, closed my eyes, then took that leap of faith, I was transformed from a boy forged by fear into a fearless man who wasn't afraid to leap into the unknown! Just as I predicted, I went down deep into the water and came up washed clean of my doubt. A feeling of accomplishment consumed me.

PROTECT YOUR INVESTMENT

Being an early entrepreneur can be both a blessing and a curse. Entrepreneurship, in its early stages, is when most have vibrant ideas, energy to follow all their passions, the creativity to continue to create new ideas or even the will to win. But what people don't talk about is the lack of support for your dreams, the late nights tossing and turning because you have so much on your mind, and early mornings getting up and working on what you thought about all night. Or, better yet, those ideas that you sit on because of the opinions of others or your doubt in your abilities as an early entrepreneur.

I have a question for you: When is the RIGHT time to turn an idea, thought, or concept into a company? The early stages of entrepreneurship remind me of the decision college athletes make about being drafted before their senior year. Many players make this decision for different reasons, however, the outcome was to take their talents to the next level and live the dream of playing professionally. There are always those special stories where athletes who are projected to go high in the draft decide to stay in college another year to either get their degree or win the national championship for their Alma Mater. There are also those stories where people go too early and don't get drafted when they expected or go to late and their once high draft projection turns into a 25th round pick.

These stories, no matter the outcome, are great because not everyone has the opportunity of being a part of the NFL or NBA draft, let alone a college athlete good enough to be considered. Have you ever seen an idea you never worked on become successful? Better yet, have you ever seen a multi-million dollar company form out of thin air after a few leisure talks with friends? I didn't think so. When Uber, the now very successful technological transportation network, had just opened their doors, a group of friends and I were sitting around pondering if Uber had a food delivery service. At the time, we were freshmen and sophomores in college. We did not have transportation to get to the restaurants we craved late at night or early in the morning. We sat and talked about the possibilities of creating a service on campus that would employ its on students and drivers. We wrote up a business plan, started to reach out to local restaurants and our early ambition begin to die down after our dream for having a consistent 24/7 food delivery service began to look a bit more difficult than our expertise.

Two years later at the beginning of the school year, rumors were spreading over all the business networks that Uber was launching Uber Eats, an online meal ordering, and delivery platform. I remember getting a call from my buddy at the time about how that had been our idea first. We laughed about it, talked about how we probably should have explored the idea more, and ended our call. But as I grew older, I learned that this was not a laughing matter. This was an example of being a step behind in the market place. From this experience, I learned more than to continue those great ideas, or follow the timing of the market, but to ride the wave until my ideas become successful. I learned the importance of protecting your idea investments and that ultimately, you do not need a master's degree to be a masterpiece.

THE DESTINED DESTINATION OF DESTINY

I'd rather make nothing and help a million people, then to make a million dollars and help nobody. Society has entangled our minds in a corporate culture where we have forgotten about true character, true value, and sticking to our morals. Let me ask you something. Would you be willing to turn down millions to hold to your morals or character? Quite often, we witness big-time CEOs and even politicians squander their souls away for coins. Around the time when I wrote this book, Wells Fargo fired 5,300 employees over opening 5 million phony accounts. Matt Egan, a journalist for CNN Money, reported, "Wells Fargo employees secretly created millions of unauthorized bank and credit card accounts without their customers knowing since 2011." It was also noted further in the article that "Wells Fargo employees secretly opened unauthorized accounts to hit sales targets and receive bonuses," Richard Corday, director of the Consumer Financial Protection Bureau.

The full scope of this scandal was not only shocking, but it was truly heartbreaking because these employees had the choice to do the right thing instead of looking for a little bit more on their bonus checks at the end of the quarter. Malcolm X said it the best, "There is nothing better than adversity. Every defeat, every heartbreak, every loss, contains its own seed, its own lesson on how to improve your performance next time." Taking it a bit further, I truly believe there's something wrong with your character if opportunity controls your loyalty.

In 2016, The United Nations Food and Agriculture Organization estimated that about 795 million people of the

7.3 billion people in the world, or one in nine, were suffering from chronic undernourishment in 2014-2016. According to Pearson, The United States has a "Cognitive skills and educational attainment" score of 0.39 which makes the United States rank fourteenth out of forty countries ranked in that category. Our educational systems are failing, there is a vast amount of gentrification taking place around our inner cities, our women and men are dying daily, and jails are being built where schools once stood. Instead of waiting for our annual corporation performance review, as people, we need to do daily, weekly, and monthly self-character reviews. There is a major disconnect between what is happening and what needs to be happening.

I remember working for a company and how at the end of the year, we did a year-end meeting or what we called an annual performance review. At this meeting, employees from all over the nation came together, and we assessed the goals, highlighted the successes, and even gave awards to the top performers. It was an amazing opportunity to network with other professionals, but also learning the strategies that others were using to be successful in their perspective territories. It was more of acknowledging the high flyers and teaching everyone else how to get on the same level of the top performers. Questions that were brought up during these meetings were as such:

Did we meet our targets? Did we grow our territories? Did we meet our objectives? Did we stick to our goals? Did we achieve essentially everything that we set out to achieve in the given year? Throughout the year, we would have monthly conference calls with the region, bi-weekly conference calls with our territory teams, and even quarterly conference calls with the whole nation. At the beginning of every year, we were required to attend a fast start meeting that was used provide us with the necessary foundation to be successful by setting new goals, assessing new standards, and being provided with new yearly objectives. Before these meetings, we had to submit an annual performance review that would ultimately determine if we were to get our bonuses, if we were to get promoted, and in some cases, if we're to get a pay increase.

Based on analytical data, whether it be quantitative or qualitative, companies use these performance metrics to see if we will be able to feed our families, maintain our lifestyles, and even put food on our tables. In life, we are always challenged to meet goals and to meet objectives.

We are always challenged to be held to a higher standard and expectation, to be better than the last day, the last quarter, the competitor product, or even beating out our colleagues and team members. We are so focused to obtain goals where we forget our company's culture, values, and the reasons why we were even interested in taking the role in the company. Warren Buffet stated, "Price is what you pay, value is what you get." So why are we focused so much on prices, dollars, and numbers instead of focusing on quality, value, and contribution?

During my time with a company, I remember being on a conference call with the Atlanta District. When I was interviewed and through the first months of onboarding into the company, there was a significant focus on the company being a Credo based company. Part of the Credo focused on making the patients the center of our attention. Well, I brought this up on a conference call as a way to remind others of the original foundation and lifeline of the company. Instead of being met with praise and understanding, I was met with a response that was geared back to the bottom-line. I was basically told not to focus on the patients, but to focus on the profit and how we could outperform competitor products. As a sales professional, we should not just be known as sharks; we should believe in what we do and build a strong enough foundation to build upon. Sales are service.

Jim Rohn quoted, "One customer well taken care of could be more valuable than $10,000 worth of advertising." Our new age business mogul and technological genius, Bill Gates, stated, "Your most unhappy customers are your greatest source of learning." Mark Cuban, American businessman, investor, author, television personality and currently the owner of the NBA's Dallas Mavericks runs his business around not just the money, but he teaches us that sales are the most important aspect of a company. Sales are in turn about how well you treat your customers and stay ahead of your customers' requirements. When we look at our lives, we go through the same types of conference call feelings that blindside, and sometimes bamboozle us. Sometimes, we are attacked from other sources or places where we lose focus on the actual mission at hand. We lose focus on the customers and, in terms of life, the people we impact each day.

At the beginning of the year, we all have those new year's resolutions, in business, they call it fast start meetings. We look at it as that gym membership we purchase to live a healthier lifestyle, the decision to leave a relationship to be happier, or

THE MISSION PLAN: THE DISCOVERY

to join a church to become more purposeful. Throughout the first quarters of the year, you see waves of people in the gym, in church, and posting memes on social media that allude to their singleness and focus on self. However, somewhere around July goals begin to fall off, and the workout "gains" pictures become few and far between. It appears that the first quarter and the last quarter of the year are when people are most focused on their goals. My question is, "What is everyone doing during the other six months?"

Do people not care anymore? Do people not stick to their schedules? Do people lose track of what their mission was? Are people blindsided, deceived, and taken off track? What causes them to lose focus? Many of us fall victim to telling the world our plan but never showing the world action. As a result, year in and year out, our goals remain the same and never take off. Our dreams remain only a figment of our imagination, and our reality, a dreary place from which we wish to escape.

A goal without a plan is just a wish. If the plan doesn't work, don't change the goal, just change the plan or the rules of engagement. We must look at life as a Garmin, and if you're not familiar with what a Garmin is, it is a reliable, full-featured GPS navigator. Garmin not only helps us get where we need to go, but it also provides the driver with alerts to help with awareness. Have we become doubtful about our dreams? Are we letting people distract us and add roadblocks to our dreams? Are we letting people pull us aside and steer us off track? You are the reliable, full-featured GPS navigation system and your goals are the route to you need to take to turn your dreams into reality. The experiences that we go through in our lives are those driver alerts that help to increase our awareness, empower our senses, and pave the way to our success. You must not take those bad experiences for granted. Instead, allow them to be learning opportunities that will set the foundation for a positive ending. As the Garmin, you must find what you need, and get where you're going with ease. You must take criticism not as personal, but as an opportunity for growth. Every time you are criticized, you are empowered, inspired, motivated and cultivated into who you were destined to be.

If you need eggs to finish that cake that you are working on at your home, milk to add to that smoothie, or butter to add to that pot before you begin cooking, you are going to stop what you are doing and head to the grocery store to pick up those items. There may be an accident at the first stop sign, a roadblock ten minutes into your trip, or even a long line at check-out to purchase the items, but because you have to finish what's on the stove, you push past those obstacles. We must adopt the same approach in our lives every single day. We need those ingredients to finish the idea that we thought about last week, last month, or even last summer. The roadblocks or experiences that we have gone through have not jolted us forward, they have kept us at the red light, and we pulled over to the side of the road. We weren't patient with our dreams because, in our head, we didn't have time for it. The reality is that those experiences didn't mean failure, it means you failed yourself. In life, we have goals, dreams, and objectives; whether that be to get in the gym, start a new diet, pass the exit exam, graduate from school, or even take that girl to prom. When we are driving on that highway towards success, there may be weather delays, traffic jams, roadblocks, or accidents slowing us down, but that doesn't mean that we won't arrive at our destination.

The day you change your destination is the day you doubt your destiny. Life is a marathon and a transformation process. We cannot expect to go to the gym on a Monday and expect results on a Tuesday. We cannot expect to get in our car and magically arrive at our destination. We cannot work hard one day and expect to obtain success on the next. Every minute, hour, and day that we work hard, is a day that we get closer and closer to the day where we begin to visualize the fruits of our labor. It's about staying committed to that plan of action, and if that plan doesn't work, we must learn how to adapt and fit within our succession plan. Henry David Thoreau quoted, "what you get by achieving your goals, is nothing compared to what you become by achieving your goals."

We appreciate the process not the accomplishment. We appreciate the hard work not the trophy. I remember listening to an interview with Allyson Felix, Olympic Gold Medalist and the most decorated Women's Track and Field Athlete of all time. In the interview, she explained that she hated every day of training and how she dreaded the next day, the next workout, the next lifting program, or the next sprint. She talked about the pain she endured during the beginning stages of her career. Felix shared with the interviewer about the nights where she would wake up with cramps and couldn't sleep because of her soreness. She went on to explain how she couldn't keep a stable relationship or even some of her friends. She went on to conclude that when she won her first Gold Medal as a sprinter in the Olympics, she understood and appreciated the late nights, early mornings, pain, loss of friends, and instability of relationships. She was grateful of the process and realized that all her hard work paid off by her consistently staying committed to her dream to be the most decorated track athlete of all time. She explained how when she came back to America, she became addicted to the work and the process. She became a student of her own success, a hard work addict and was strung out on success. She understood the quote by Jim Rohn, "Discipline is the bridge between goals and accomplishments."

We are not going to see that Gold Medal at the beginning, we are not going to see that full bank account, we are not going to see that perfect body on the first day in the gym, but every single day that we work at it, it begins to get clearer and clearer. Over time, when we look in the mirror, into our accounts, or around our necks, we see that all of our hard work paid off.

WHY THE PROCESS IS MORE REWARDING THAN THE PRODUCT

As entrepreneurs, we sometimes forget how important the processes are in our business and in our lives. The product may have the highest financial reward in terms of business success, but it is always the processes that are the most rewarding in the success of our lives. The process is a series of actions or steps taken in order to achieve a particular end. In business we may look at this as setting goals, setting deadlines and having quarterly and even annual reviews to assess the progress. Over the course of a year, it is the small daily, weekly, monthly and quarterly wins that get us to the point

THE MISSION PLAN: THE DISCOVERY

where we look back and assess if we had a successful year. Whatever your profession, effective process planning is key to reducing time, effort and money to achieving your goal. A plan in life or business serves as the map to get to your destination.

HOW DOES THE PROCESS WORK?
1. Develop objectives
2. Develop tasks to meet those objectives
3. Determine resources needed to implement tasks
4. Create a timeline
5. Determine tracking and assessment method
6. Finalize plan
7. Distribute to all involved in the process

TRUST THE PROCESS

The process of being a successful entrepreneur is absolutely amazing. As I was sitting in my bed as my son was sleeping I could feel the energy focused on one dream and no matter of how hard it takes me to get there, I was willing to make the sacrifices. One thing that I have newly learned is that you have to be willing to make sacrifices at any time, knowing that the outcome will be worth it in the long run. You have to be willing to sacrifice what you want now, for what you want most in the future. In this newly formed digital world, everyone sees the public glory, but it is the private sacrifices that are required to reach true success. The challenges you overcome, the lessons you learn on the way, the mistakes, trials, and tribulations are all a part of you growing, maturing, and becoming what you are destined to being. It is more important to just slow down and gain the lessons you are needing along the journey then to rush the process and arrive at your destination empty. Trust the process, what you thought was your destruction was really setting you up for your direction.

NEVER STOP LEARNING

Never stop learning, because life itself never stops teaching. I was listening to a late night podcast from one of my mentors, David Shands and he was telling his listeners to; Wipe those tears off our faces right then at that very moment. He went on to explain as part of the journey of entrepreneurship to not let the loses lie to you. The loses will lead you to believe you are losing but you are not losing, you are just learning. You have to take those lessons that you learned from the losses and leverage them to win. Malcolm X quoted, "Education is the passport to the future, for tomorrow belongs to those who prepare for it today." The world is an educational institution and every experience and everyone in it is a teacher. Make sure when you wake up in the morning, you go to school and get your daily life lesson.

THE MISSION PLAN: THE DISCOVERY

Part of growth is looking at every opposition as an opportunity and every loss as a learning opportunity for growth. For thirty days, I want you to write down one thing you learned during that day. Whether it be about yourself, about other people, or about the world around you. For thirty days, I want you to turn every situation into a foundation of knowledge.

TIPS FOR SUCCESS

The first step to realizing how to jump is realizing that jumping starts with YOU taking the first step forward.

When we are driving on that highway towards success, there may be weather delays, traffic jams, roadblocks, or accidents slowing us down, but that doesn't mean that we won't arrive at our destination.

If the plan doesn't work, don't change the goal, just change the plan or the rules of engagement.

In order to become who you are mean to be, you have to sacrifice who you currently are.

We have to produce more than we consume. Change our thinking from what is the world doing for me, to what can I do for the world?

"The essence of strategy is choosing what NOT to do."
– Michael Porter

CHAPTER FIVE
THE BACKSEAT DRIVERS

At some time in our lives, we've all experienced a backseat driver. If you haven't you're probably it. The backseat driver is typically the DJ, GPS, and Trip Scheduler on long road trips and even short trips down the street. Though they are not in the driver's seat, they give instructions, making commentary, and may even critique the driver, as if they are driving. The funny thing about the backseat driver is that they make everything conducive to their desires. They adjust (or instruct) changes for the air, they play the music they KNOW and want to hear, they request stops when they are hungry or need to use the restroom. Backseat drivers typically have little to no concern for anyone else in the car. This is how they receive the title, Backseat Driver. While backseat driver may provide humor or something to rant about during a long drive, you must be careful not to allow the backseat drivers in your circle to control your life. This, my friend, is not a laughing matter.

THE MISSION PLAN: THE DISCOVERY

In life, it's not okay for us to let passengers drive our lives. These navigators often have much critique but provide very little support. They will often attempt to set the temperature of your life and tell you when is a good time to do something. Additionally, they are known to make suggestions about where you should stop on your path to success. In life, backseat drivers say things like, "Okay, that's enough. You don't have to work that hard!" Or, "Who do you think you are? You're just like everybody else." Or, "I don't think that is a smart idea; nobody is going to buy that for you." Or, "Your best bet is to get a good job and wait until you have saved up enough money to try that." The backseat driver is a distraction if nothing else, and we cannot allow them to take control of the destination.

Being distracted isn't an action, it is more so of a process or a series of actions performed to achieve a certain ending or, in this case, not to achieve a certain level of achievement. Distraction is the process of diverting the attention of an individual or group from a desired area of focus. When this happens, it, in turn, blocks the gathering or the reception of valuable information. It's like trying to type an email or a text, but someone keeps interrupting you. After you give them your attention, you forget everything you planned to type. It's also like turning around to talk to a friend during class, only to turn back around and realize you've missed very important directions. Many people are lost in their lives because they have allowed distractions, the outside noise, and the commentators dictate their outcome and achievements. Greg McKeown, author of the New York Times Bestseller, Essentialism: The Disciplined Pursuit of Less talks about applying systematic discipline for discerning what is absolutely essential, then eliminating everything that is not, so we can make the highest possible contribution towards the things that really matter. He writes in the book that by forcing us to apply more selective criteria for what is essential, the disciplined pursuit of less empowers us to reclaim control of our own choices about where to spend our precious time and energy – instead of giving others the implicit permission to choose for us.

Growing up, I allowed many people to control, dictate, and run my life, emotions, decisions, and actions. I was never focused on essentials or priorities because I wanted to fit everything into my schedule and please everyone. As a result, I became overwhelmed, less productive, and extremely frustrated all of the time. The quality of my work suffered as well. One day, a mentor pulled me to the side to chat with me about the direction I was headed in.

"Kyle, do you like being courted?" he asked.

"Dr. Smith, I really don't know what you mean by that," I said puzzled.

"What is it that you want? Do you just like to pursue any opportunity and enjoy the feeling of being in front of crowds and shining?" he inquired.

"Not really," I said. "Well, sort of. I'm not sure, Dr. Smith. Why do you ask?"

He went on to explain how in life, there is an optimization level for everything. "You must begin to prioritize your life, Kyle," he explained. "Because if you don't, your life will begin to be prioritized by all of the companies, all of the opportunities, or even all of the things you said yes to. With

THE MISSION PLAN: THE DISCOVERY

your degree, with your GPA, with the University you are graduating from, under all of the constraints, what is the best possible outcome that you want to have when selecting a position after school? In terms of salary, benefits, company culture, location, traveling, etc...." I had never been asked this question, so I didn't know how to answer at the time. Then, he posed another question, "Now let's talk about the bare minimum. What do you need to have? How much money will you need to survive and what are the most essential and most important things to you when selecting the position?"

His questions made me think about the difference between what I wanted and what I actually needed to be successful. You will never get to a state of true happiness and success if you continue to let the wants in life distract you from what you truly need.

Robert Ingersoll once quoted, "The only way we rise, is by lifting others." Has so much changed since the 1800s when Robert Green "Bob" Ingersoll said this in the courtyard during the later stages of the Civil War? Have we lost our way as a human race where we are more concerned about the next technological innovation instead of being concerned about the outcome of our children's futures? Bob, nicknamed as The Great Agnostic, was frequently poked at by the earlier press in this century, but still advocated freethought and humanism through his speeches on subjects as broad as Shakespeare to Reconstruction. His most popular subjects were agnosticism and the sanctity and refuge of the family. His very radical views on religion, slavery, woman's suffrage, and other issues during this era of evangelism prevented him from pursuing or holding political offices higher than that of state attorney general. He didn't believe in withholding information from the public. He wanted to increase the standard of living for all citizens through his vigorous defense of the need of basic human rights.

Although "The Great Agnostic" wasn't an athlete and didn't lift in the modern-day sense, through him being an abolitionist, American lawyer, Civil War veteran, political leader, and orator, he was the one doing the heavy lifting in terms of people and uplifting through one of his most famous quotes, "There are in nature neither rewards nor punishments, there are consequences." What are the consequences when we choose not to carry the weight of others? What do you think could happen if you began to wonder how much of what weighs you down is not your weight to carry? When we try to carry the weight of the world, we are reminded that we only have two hands gifted to us by God.

At times, we don't realize the weight of something we've been carrying until we feel the weight release and we begin to feel free from strife, independent from illusions, and allow achievements to activate in your life. Regardless if you are lifting five pounds of past or one hundred pounds of disappointment, the art and practice of weight lifting can help you improve and maintain fitness through failure, strength through tough situations, and empower endurance.

Many people that I have come across think they are killing it in their lives, just as many people believe they are killing it in the gym throwing the weight back, screaming, and making those unnecessary grunting noises during their workout. In life, it is the excessive clothing, materials, houses that people can't afford, or merely the falsehoods of what success really is and looks like. The reality of it is that many are not as effective as they could be. One of the major components that determines success is the execution through each rep in the gym and execution of each goal in life. Thomas Edison quoted, "Vision without execution is delusion." Execution, is everything and it is not just about the strategy, it is about the execution of the strategy. The technique or the strategic plan is also a big factor that can influence your injury risk, but most important, it will determine if all your hard work results in you ultimately looking like Captain Achievement or the Wonder Woman of opportunity.

TIPS TO LIFE WEIGHT LIFTING
Rest

In our society, it appears that we are never expected to rest. We are expected to always be on the go. We look at rest and relaxation as some form of guilt or laziness, and the thought of doing nothing is a sin to people growing their careers. We say things like, "If you're not working, your dying." Or, my personal favorite, "You can sleep when you're dead." In this day and age, people glorify burning the midnight oil, operating off very little hours of sleep, and running off of energy drinks and coffee. It appears that unless you're chugging three cups of coffee or four energy drinks, you're not working hard enough. Some people even have the nerve to shake their heads at entrepreneurs who take the weekend off. However, I pose this question, "If all we do is work, when will we enjoy the fruits of our hard labor?" Don't get me wrong, at certain times during the establishment and even the operation of your dreams, you will work late nights and early mornings to get things done. This is especially true for early entrepreneurs working hard to get things off the ground. Quite honestly, I know all too well that is difficult to rest when your mind is buzzing with ideas and excitement about what's to come. However, we must find time in our lives to rest. It is not just important to take a break and rest, but it is great for our mind and body. Studies show that sleep and rest are very much essential to setting the foundation for our body and minds. Growing up, my teacher would always mention that the mind is sharper if you take naps after studying. It helps your ability to retain information. Rest helps you become a stronger learner, and it trains your mind over time to trim the fat of the accessories and keep what's necessary.

The whole idea of pushing your body into hyperdrive is a myth. Healthwise, usually digestive malfunctions occur, like gas, bloating, or just the feelings of bad imbalance in our systems. In life, the imbalance is frustration, lack of quality in our work, and aggravation. I don't know about you, but none of these feelings are good feelings. These are all caused by the lack of rest. Instead of going straight to the gym after a long shift at work, maybe take a minute and read to clear your mind and calm down. Instead of knocking out that whole research paper in one night, maybe watch an episode of your favorite show to take your mind off the stress that will come with the task. Instead of coming home and getting right in the bed with your spouse, maybe just ask how his or her day went, sit on the couch, and just breath.

It is time for you to stop internalizing all that negativity and get back in touch with your mind, body, and emotions. You must become the best version of yourself and that all starts with resting that powerful mind of yours so that in return, it can produce quality life-changing work.

Avoid exhausting the muscle.

Kurt Vonnegut quoted, "Laughter and tears are both responses to frustration and exhaustion. I myself prefer to laugh, since there is less cleaning up to do afterward." There comes a time when you must learn to be less available to certain projects, people, and potential plans. Stop engaging in activities that you can't perform at the possible best of your abilities and begin to empower that entrepreneurial energy. During workouts, trainers teach their trainees to avoid pre-exhausting target muscles before working a major one. In life, we tell people to stop majoring in minor things. If you don't believe me, believe Jim Rohn's quote, "Most people fail in life because they major in minor things." If it is a secondary muscle group during a back movement, or even if it is a secondary priority through a strategic plan, you will ultimately fail to get the most out of your workout towards success if the muscle responsible for pulling the weight is too tired to assist you.

It is so easy to be focused on everything where we never truly master anything. But living a life of smarter priorities, more focus, and understanding the essentials is one of the best ways to become much more efficient and to make the most of your time. Stop running like a chicken with its head chopped off. Slowly begin to walk into your purpose and do it with power this time around. Stop overthinking what your priorities are and consistently stick to the priorities that you have set for yourself. Stop overcomplicating the essential things in life and be realistic with yourself, your schedule, and your lifestyle. Live your priorities! It is one thing to set them, but it is another to actually live them, commit to them, and make them a part of who you are.

Lift to ¾ of maximum weight.

Tim Ferris once said, "Focus on being productive, instead of busy." Productive leaders take time to empower each member of their team, whereas busy leaders don't have the time to delegate. Productive leaders are strategic thinkers, whereas busy leaders are not strategic and think poorly. Productive leaders focus on the person, the issue, the meeting, the solution, whereas busy leaders are easily distracted by technology, meetings, or other staff. Productivity is results, busy is workload and the act of filling time with tasks rather than prioritizing results. Stop trying to lift 100% of your maximum weight and work smart – not in overdrive. During this workout of life, it is okay to drop the weight and focus on higher reps, great form technique, and gaining quality results over time. The goal is to be challenged, not exhausted and changed, not extinct.

In business, productivity is the ability of any organization to utilize or leverage the available resources to innovate profitable goods or services as desired by customers. According to Forbes Magazine, productiveness increases the overall efficiency of an organization. A lot of companies only focus on being effective or efficient, but the great companies obsess over productivity, not efficiency. Productivity aligns with strategy, mission planning, and effective execution of the mission.

Use proper form.

Have you ever been working hard in the gym and during a specific exercise it feels like you may have strained or pulled a muscle? At the time, you may think, "It's just muscle soreness," but then over the next few days, it starts to become worse, and by the end of the week, it is a painful feeling that you have never felt before? What do you usually do to soothe this pain? The younger readers may say, "I'll be alright, it'll pass over time. No pain, no gain." But the older readers may have a different response that sounds like, "I'm getting old. I need to slow down. I am going to stop by the store and pick up some BENGAY or maybe take a few days off."

Have you ever experienced pain while working through life? Have you ever felt the pain of a broken heart, betrayal, disappointment, loss of a friend, spouse, or job? Will the answer that you thought about giving earlier be the same during these real-life examples? I don't think so. The feeling that comes from injury during a workout is contributed to improper form and focusing on the speed instead of the technique. In life, we experience the same thing. Our improper form is being unaware, uneducated, or even ignorant to the possibilities of getting hurt because we are so focused on rushing through the works of life that we forget about the importance of patience and technique.

When we lift heavy weights with the improper form, the body can become misaligned, and that can affect our tendons. In life, when we lift things the wrong way, we miss opportunities or potential positions. This can ultimately lead to stress, many tears, and failure. Whether we play a sport or a musical instrument, the competitive nature of life forces us to find ourselves quickly, and the tenacity and concentration that we must display. When we are forced into competition, it adds quality anxiety, stress of competitions, and the pressure to perform. This is a recipe for disaster.

We must stop coping and begin to challenge ourselves to change. We must stop focusing on the temporary fix and search for the preventative drugs of life. Studies show that when athletes suffer repeated injuries during a career, this causes maximum exposure. Physical therapist, Jonathan Reynolds, discusses how this is the point at which a person's muscles, tendons, ligaments, and tissue have reached the limit of their capabilities. It is at this point that we might become chronically injured or suffer from pervasive pain and fatigue. It is not uncommon for significant stress and trauma to occur in soft tissue, resulting in tissue destruction and loss of function.

I call this peak exertion, where you have over-worked yourself and come to the peak of what you have to give. Looking at the wider picture, we lead busy lives. Some of us have multiple jobs, children, and many responsibilities. We try to deal with stresses such as aging parents, growing children, and keeping up with the bills. As we continue to strive for success, we often don't sleep well, and we may not have the time to perform like we once did. The purpose of the proper form and learning how to prevent instead of just curing is vital to our ability to extend the life cycle of quality performance. It is not about preparing for injury; it is about understanding that it is possible to avoid disappointment, frustration, or failure with a prescription of prioritizing. Stop putting band aids on wounds that deserve treatment.

Timing

Timing! Timing! The timing of the lift is the last key to this equation to working out properly in life. Timing is important in every aspect of your life. I am sure you have heard this phrase many times, "Timing is everything." There is so much truth in that statement whether you are working out in a gym, cooking in the kitchen, striving at your company, or just sitting around with friends laughing and joking. There is evidence that suggests that increasing the velocity of the lifting phase leads to an increase in strength. When preparing that medium-well filet mignon, it is all about the timing that you have the meat on the grill. Take it off too soon, and you could end up eating raw meat. Take it off too late, and you could be eating a brick of charcoal. If your company is declining in stock valuation, they are going through layoffs, and are downsizing; it wouldn't be the right time to ask your boss for that raise that you have been waiting for during the past four months. The power of pause and proper timing when telling jokes could be the difference between a genuine joke and something that comes off as inappropriately offensive. An inappropriate pause or timing could kill the same joke.

Timing covers every aspect of your life personally and professionally. Understanding the power of proper timing when you are working out in life will be the difference of gaining the results that you want or wasting your time and resources. It is not about the timing of the market in business and investing; it is about the time in the market. When you invest in a stock and when you sell the stock will make the ultimate difference between whether you are making or losing money in the long run. Understanding the process of buying and selling or even borrowing or not borrowing could potentially be the difference between you being financially independent or financially dependent.

The moral of this timing thesis is that you need to be patient, work steady, and stay sharp. The journey to success and gaining the results you have been working for is a marathon, not a sprint. Productivity is different than being busy just as success is different from failure. Timing is the prevention that could save you from continuing to live by those bad habits that have kept you from maximizing your full potential. Your timing, even when taking medication, is very important. Taking medicine as directed is helpful in the treatment process. If you skip doses or in life skip experiences, it loses its effectiveness, and you could continue to go through the same trials and tribulations. If you take extra doses and rush your success, it can be fatal and lead to failure.

Success spotting

Spotting, by definition, is the act of supporting another person during a particular exercise, with an emphasis on allowing the participant to lift or push more than they could normally do safely. I've given you the techniques and some quick tips for weightlifting, but there are still times when a lot weighs you down, and we make the choice to push through it instead of just lightening the load. Maybe we are lifting for bulk instead of lean muscle, so we are pushing through four reps instead of twelve. You have the option of taking the weight off, or you can get people who can properly spot you. If the weight is too much, surround yourself with people who are willing to be your support system and can properly spot you through these heavy times in the gym. We are not going to be that strong at all times, but to continue to grow and get to the next level or, in this case, the next weight class, become vulnerable to your support system and let the successful be your supporters.

Take time to ask yourself a few questions. What value is this decision bringing to my life? How will my actions this make me a better person? What are my top priorities in life? Where is most of my time going? Are my decisions my decisions or are they influenced by other factors? What brings me the most happiness? If all my bills were paid every month, what would I spend my time doing? Am I the one lifting, or am I being uplifted?

The Pebble that Changed the World

When you drop any new idea in the pond of the world, regardless of how small the idea, you create a ripple effect. You have to be aware that you will be creating a cascade of change. In life, I have always strived to be the pebble in the pond that creates the ripple for change. I wanted to be the ripple effect that was committed to transforming the world around me. But before I could change the world around me, I learned the importance of first learning how to transform myself. Everything great that I have been blessed to have, blessed to learn, or even blessed to be granted with never came at a time where I was comfortable. The old ways of certain habits didn't open new doors to the possibility.

As we constantly move in life, everything we do and think affects not only ourselves but the people in our lives and their reactions, in turn, affect others. The decisions we make, the choices, and each cause has an effect. Each individual as a part of the human race has a far-reaching capacity to change the world in small ways that could ultimately massively impact the world. Our thoughts, our actions, and our decisions are like pebbles dropped in a pond and they create ripples that travel outward throughout the world.

For 25 years I was so focused on what I wanted to be when I grew up that I never took the time to think about what more I truly had to offer to the world, outside of my profession. It wasn't until I actually turned 25 where there was a drastic change in my vantage point from my perspective of life itself. Those dreams were not materials anymore, they were no longer luxuries or things that I could purchase. My aspirations no longer had a price tag, yet they had a purpose. I was no longer focused on what I wanted to be when I grew up; I was focused on what I wanted to become and how I wanted to be remembered.

I was at lunch with a friend of mine and during lunch, he grabbed the napkin and drew a dot in the middle of the napkin. He explained to me that I was the dot on the napkin and the napkin represented our current city that we were living in. He drew a large circle that didn't fill up the napkin, however, it covered a lot of distance. He said imagine this dot is your pebble and the circle around the pebble is the impact that you have left in the city. He said there is still space left because it still leaves room for growth and for you to continue to spread your wings and touch other people. He then proceeded in opening the napkin all the way up and now it showed my dot get even smaller and the once circle that covered the majority of the napkin, now covered only a fourth of the whole napkin. He said now Kyle, the napkin being open represents the state that we live in. He went on and on about how many ripples I had based upon how big the pebble, or how big of an impact that I had left in the world. In the pond of possibility, I welcome you to ask yourself how big is your pebble? It is said, that a life is not important except in the impact it has on others lives. So I also welcome you to ask yourself, how much have you impacted your family, community, state or world? So many times I have thought about who and what I needed in order for me to get to the place that I wanted to be in my life; where all along I've learned that the purpose of life is for us to think about who and what we could be for others.

CHALLENGE

Over the next three weeks, schedule time to do the following to increase your life satisfaction. Happiness begins and ends with you. There is no circumstance, no situation, no mistake, trial or tribulation that should take you away from the internal happiness that we all seek and most definitely deserve. Make the choice today that no matter what life throws at you, you will CHOOSE your happiness.

1. Read Your Favorite Novel
2. Setting and Exceeding Goals
3. Maintaining Close Social Relationships
4. Indulge in Small Pleasures
5. Get Involved in Community Service

TIPS FOR SUCCESS

Time is the first form of currency, spend it wisely.

It's not about quantity over quality nor is it about quality over quantity. Focus on producing a quantity of quality.

Silence the noise and accelerate towards your success.

SECTION THREE
THE DESTINY

Everyone has a purpose in life, no matter the environment or circumstances, everyone has a unique set of gifts or talents that serve an intricate part of the universe. Your story is not your own; it is a gift meant to be given away to the masses. The biggest challenge is being authentic and understanding the importance of your brand. During this journey, The Mission Plan: The Destiny, you will learn how to release all the grief, heartbreak, and pain on your platform towards purpose. It is time for you to live your life as a miraculous expression of divinity, not just on occasions, but in every moment, in every breath, and every step moving forward in your life. When your actions and passions align, you will move into purposeful destiny. Through stories, examples, and exercises, you'll be taught how expressing your unique talents will ultimately lead to fulfilling the needs of the world. The very purpose of our lives is to seek happiness. This section will equip you with the tools to become carefree, joyful, and happy.

LET'S WORK

I read in a book once that no oppressor is going to give you the kind of education that results in them losing their land and power...

So I've always been curious on why
our people are so motivated to put down the books to pick up the remote to watch the Love and Hip Hops, Housewives of Atlanta or TV series like Power.

Now we have a whole generation of men
who are more concerned with the profits, instead of being prophets, leading to our young men knowing nothing but how to be courageous cowards.

These same young men are coming to their woman's home to enjoy her physical gifts and presents, but never her emotional presence, leading to a bunch of men who are bounded by the bedroom, still emotionally lost, wearing a smile with a knife in their heart looking like a Halloween costume.

But now let me talk from a different perspective.

Not from a place of stereotypical statistic because I believe that what we do in life will echo into eternity.

THE MISSION PLAN: THE DESTINY

We've moved past the metal shackles, now our culture is bound by debt, educational failure, and wage disparity. Throw our hands up, they still shoot.

Then send our brothers and sisters to the prison system creating the next wave of modern slavery.

Tonight is going to be that night,
where a new foundation is laid.

But we first have to understand that
we are living in an Information Age;
Where technology rules our thoughts
and machines control our days.

The hurtful truth about information
Is that it creates speculation

Instead of facts thoroughly thought out
through study, self-investment, and proper education.

They don't teach us about theoretical
education

Instead, we are taught to be entrepreneurial
employees through employment and innovation.

But this mindset that has been created

Stems from a capitalist mindset

LET'S WORK

Indoctrinated into our minds, spirits, and
even into our races.
Now economic gaps, lack of resources,
and gentrification rule our nation.

But what is information? It's nothing but speculation,
thoughts, opinions, and man's definition of media content or declaration.

It is a limitless pill that keeps us
limited from our human nature.

We are so quick to negatively comment but never
conscious on our own detrimental behaviors.

True power is in resilience,
education, and uniting with our neighbor.

Regardless of your color, race, gender,
Ethnicity, or religious background.

Don't you ever forget that you are
Kings and Queens standing amongst giants;
Don't ever let a small failure break you down.

You are worth more than wealth
And your job on earth is more than a salary.

It's bigger than that investment portfolio,
401K Plan, or what they decided to pay you hourly.

THE MISSION PLAN: THE DESTINY

This night is dedicated to you,
The dreamer, the believer, the critical thinker.
The engineer working on that block chain technology or even that aspiring singer.

This night is dedicated to you,
The single mother and the single father.
We can't give up now just because
we have it a little harder.

In a world filled with violence, hatred, and societal stereotypes, I dedicate this night to the leaders in this room that can't sleep because their visions continue to keep them up at night.

We must stop being so focused on
securing the bag and nothing else.

Because I'm telling you right now that you
are the bag, so secure yourself!

Let's WORK!

INTRODUCTION
LOCKER ROOM OF LOVE

At the beginning of my speaking career, while working with students and business professionals around the country, I would always relate my messages to sports or fashion because those were topics most people could relate to. Now, there are still many people who have never been athletes or don't follow fashion. If you are one of those people, I believe this message will still relate to you. Even if you have no idea what a foul, goal, or rebound is, I'm more than positive that you are familiar with the term, locker room. A locker room is where athletes and coaches go before workouts, practice, games, or competitions to change clothes, relax, or just sit down and examine the team's performance. However, for most athletes, it is more than a room to store personal belongings. It is a place of serenity. It is where bonds are built with teammates. It is where they receive inspirational talks and motivation from the head coaches. In college, as a track athlete, I never had that locker room feel. In a sport like track, swimming, or even tennis, athletes are responsible for being disciplined, accountable, and committed to his or her skill during competition. Athletes in individual sports overall success are their own, but so is their disappointment — a combination that can quickly build confidence, self-esteem, coping skills and resilience.

As a track athlete, during competitions, I learned to think independently, make adjustments, solve problems, and resolve conflicts on my feet. I loved being held accountable for my success or failure. At times, however, I missed the motivating and comforting feeling that you get from being a part of a team. The feeling of being on a team is valuable. Your work and effort never go unnoticed; it is always appreciated. Also, on a team, you can't just be replaced instantly because you are part of the system your coaches have built around you. A team is a unit. It holds every member accountable for each other's success. Together teammates figure out solutions to every problem that may arise. An African Proverb quotes, "If you want to go fast, go alone. If you want to go far, go together." Through life, at times, we are so focused on speeding to get to the finish line. We want to be first to graduate high school, first to get into class and sit down, first to answer the question, first to graduate college, first to get the job, first to get the promotion. We always equate being first to success. Have you ever stopped to think, "Why the rush?"

In our culture, we have always been taught to be the best and to be first at everything we do. When we are overly determined to be the best, we miss the opportunity to develop the mindset needed for success. Being the best is a fixed mindset, the belief that your basic qualities, intelligence, talents, abilities are enough to be great or, in your case, being the base. Everyone has a certain amount, and that is that. The success mindset is having a growth mindset and the belief that even basic talents and abilities can be developed over time through experience, mentorship, support, and resiliency. Successful people are not worried about how great they look, how smart they are, or being first. The success mindset looks through a different lens and constantly strives to grow. A growth mindset is key to boosting our sense of self-worth, enjoying the process of learning, and improving the quality of your life. Through a fixed mindset, the first feeling of failure, disappointment, or inadequacy will force you in a state of insecurity, depression, and heartbreak. You were too focused on the loss and not the lesson to be learned.

Whether we currently possess the success mindset or are trapped in our fixed mindset, when we fall short, who teaches us how to carve our mountains of mistakes into monuments of success? Through our many defeats, who gives us direction? In our shortcomings, who gives us support? When we collapse, who catches us and cultivates our character with conviction and consideration?

If you're trying to lose body fat in the workout of life, you can't continue to eat the sweets in the snack room at work, indulge in the pizza parties, and attend the ice cream socials at your university. You may find it hard staying on track and staying focused on what you are trying to accomplish if you continue to surround yourself by people or situations that contribute to your setbacks instead of your breakthroughs. To be successful, you need to recruit supporters of all kinds

THE MISSION PLAN: THE DESTINY

and start to build that Locker Room of Love. Your problems are not insoluble, your mistakes are not monsters, and your failures are fixable. However, it begins with what is placed in the backdrop of your masterpiece. It is time for you to be elevated by your environment, backed up by what's in the background, and motivated by your milieu.

Finding your locker room of love is not similar to anything else you can find these days in social media, mobile applications, internet, and technology. Sometimes, your biggest supporters are the people you've been through life with and have actually met face to face. One of the best ways to stay on track with your success lifestyle is to tell your friends and family about your goals, dreams, and aspirations. This is the initial assessment for who will be on your practice team and who won't even make the cut. I am a firm believer that people shouldn't be allowed at the table when you are eating if they didn't help you pick the groceries. If they are not willing to support you through the process, they shouldn't be able to enjoy your company when you are successful. This is when we begin to trim the fat instead of having a bunch of fatty acids surrounding us. We need to have people who are supportive of our future achievements. So, begin asking around. You'll never know what you may find. There is maybe a friend who is walking on the same journey that you are walking and you both are walking alone. Finding a consistent elevation partner helps make you more accountable on this passageway to perfection and quality performance.

Yes, you need more than just the support of your friends and family to be successful. In these cases, you may search for mentors or sponsorships that you need to achieve and, most importantly, maintain the motivation as you are climbing the mountain. Education goes further than what is taught in the classroom by way of formal education. It is vital to be surrounded by valuable mentors, coaches, and external teachers. Mentors serve as the ACE while you play the cards life has dealt you. According to researchers, the word ace comes from the Old French word as (from Latin 'as') meaning 'a unit,' from the name of a small Roman Coin. Historically, the ace had the lowest value, and this still holds in many popular European games. But in this game we call life, the more ACE's you have, the more success you will experience.

THE A.C.E. MODEL

Awareness

Chinese teacher, editor, politician, and philosopher of the Spring and Autumn period of Chinese history, Confucius, quoted, "True wisdom is knowing what you don't know." You cannot expand your thinking if you don't know what you don't know. A mentor brings awareness to unknown topics and can teach you new ways to do things or bring about changes to increase your current efficiency and ability. He or she may recognize where you are falling short and be willing to teach you. A great mentor is not selfish; they are selfless and remember how they were when they were just starting in their careers. They are willing to take you under their wing and serve as the support you need to succeed. They aren't only aware; they are accountable and don't see mentoring as just "a thing to do." They are committed and willing to continually share information and ongoing support to you during the good and the bad times.

Character

In the early 1900s, Dwight Eisenhower quoted, "The qualities of a great man are vision, integrity, courage, understanding, the power of articulation, and profundity of character." These same qualities are expected in the pursuit of a great mentor. Willingness to share, knowledge, and expertise are all qualities great mentors possess. They exhibit the personal attributes it takes to be successful in the field. They serve as a positive role model and demonstrate a positive attitude by showing you what it takes to be productive and successful. The demonstration of specific behavior and actions required in this field are critical to setting the foundation for providing guidance and constructive feedback. It is hard to take constructive criticism from one who has never constructed anything. This will be your opportunity to grow by identifying current strengths and weaknesses that can be sharpened. It's about challenging your mind, not just providing you with all the answers.

Example

Matthew Mellon quoted, "Intuition is the number one tool in the toolbox." It's time for you to build with actions instead of continuing to use words and just talk. I'm sure you and your next-door neighbors probably have toolboxes or even first aid kits somewhere in your home. Unless you guys are best friends and go to the same store and purchase all your products at the same time, your neighbor probably has different tools in his garage than the ones you have in yours. Great mentors can share shortcuts, back ways, and networks with you. It's like that taxi driver that takes a detour, so you don't hit traffic en route to your destination. The mentor serves as the taxi driver and can provide you with alternative routes to get to your destination. Just as the taxi driver teaches you the alternative way, a mentor is often someone who pours knowledge back into someone. Great mentors lead by example and usually are well respected among their colleagues and employees at all levels of the organization, community group, or network. You will look at this person as a role model. You could potentially see yourself filling the mentor's role in the future.

NO RETREAT + NO SURRENDER = SUCCESS

Letting people go doesn't mean you hate them, it just means that you love yourself. This is the first step in building that locker room of love. You are the commander of your mission and the captain of your ship. You give direction to your destiny. Stop wasting your energy, time, and feelings on people who don't value them. The problems we go through aren't waiting for us to be ready for them; they are usually standing at the front door awaiting our arrival.

Building that foundation of supporters shifts the weather and the storm blows off the roof in our lives, we will have that foundation of love that keeps us standing strong. Stop worrying about the windows and the fence of your home and focus on setting a forceful foundation. When we relieve ourselves from the weary and the weak, we develop strength within ourselves. We become prepared for that moment when the light of opportunity shines yet again on the horizon. Any organization, business, school, household, and life is as good as its leadership. Now, this can be twofold. On one hand, we need leaders that we serve, and on the other hand, we have to be great leaders that people follow. The art of great communication is the language of leadership, and being able to effectively communicate to people sets the foundation for a great leader. Simon Sinek, a successful author, motivational speaker, and marketing consultant, has the formula for what makes a great leader. He suggests, it's someone who makes their employees feel secure, who draws staffers into a circle of trust. But creating trust and safety – especially in an uneven economy – means taking on big responsibility. It's about employees being inspired or empowered to act or take responsibility for their actions or quality of work; it is not about employees doing the work so they don't lose their job or just to get that promotion.

One of my college professors would always tell me about the story of a captain and burned ships. This, by far, is one of the best stories of leadership that I have ever listened to, and I still hold it with me to this day. The story, as told by my professor, took place in 1519. Captain Hernan Cortes landed in Veracruz to begin his great conquest. Upon arriving, he gave the order to his men to burn down all the ships. When he told the story, I was puzzled, and in shock that he wouldn't at least leave one ship just in case the conquest wasn't successful or in the event of an emergency. At that same moment, I realized that I had missed the point and it wasn't about Captain Cortes' action to burn the ships, it was the principle that retreat is easy when you have the option, and either he was going to succeed or die on that island.

The longer we postpone our actions, the more time fear has to consume our futures. Retreat shouldn't be an option, and if we truly want to achieve the level of success in which we each desire, there are times when we need to "burn the ships" on the shore. The questions that we need to ask ourselves are: What are we afraid to let go of? What ships (in our lives) only serve as excess inventory? What makes these ships so hard to burn? Is it a sense of false security or false obligation? Is it an unknown fear or our perception of failure? I can't answer those questions for you, but just as Captain Cortes, you must be on a mission. The only way to keep yourself and your locker room of love from quitting on the mission is to take retreat off the table.

MANAGEMENT MISCONCEPTION

For those who take the opportunity, college is the best time of any individual's life. College is the only place you can try out different career paths, majors, classes, interests, and even have the ability to intern and try out different companies and jobs. By the time you graduate, you can fully know what direction you want to go into.

As an intern, I remember riding in the car with my boss on our way back to the office after lunch and listening to how he talked to his employees and colleagues; it was so astonishing. It was as if he were talking to his children and not adults. I was just a student at the time, but as an adult, I don't know how I would have handled conversations where I was disrespected, talked down to, and belittled. I could feel the tension in that phone call from sitting in the passenger seat. When we sat in board meetings, he would not acknowledge new ideas or accept feedback. He was more of a communist dictator than a manager invested in his workforce's development and wellbeing. I call this behavior "The Curse of the Corner Office." Professionals often look at the corner office as superiority and believe their title gives them authority. The reality is that it doesn't matter if you are a senior-level executive or an entry-level associate; the success of any organization is predicated on the manager's development of and investment in the organization.

The workplace is not a dictatorship; it is a democracy. Your employees must feel like they are contributing citizens of society or, in business, valuable assets to the company. We are only as good as our employees, our workforce, and our sales team. They are the lifeline of each organization. Many times, supervisors and management try to give executive orders instead of being leading executives. Managers are the reason companies soar or sink. As entrepreneurs or business professionals, we must understand that employees are the backbone of any organization. Management means accountability, not control. A good manager's top priority is developing employees and helping them to become better. Referring to yourself as an entrepreneur does not make you an entrepreneur; your actions do. As managers, our titles don't give us control. Our development of our employees gives us our credibility and builds trust among our employees.

I once helped a group of managers understand how to establish a team environment when there wasn't one in place. Before I built a strategy for the managers, I wanted to meet their employees and all the people they would work with in any way for their business. What I received from the employees was a complete disconnect from what I observed listening to the mangers and their expectations. The employees didn't feel valuable, nor did they feel appreciated for the work they were producing. In many of the conversations I had with the various employees, many of them said the management team didn't even know them or take the time to get to know them. They were more so dictators instead of concerned for the professional development of employees. At this same company, there was such a high turnover rate of both managers and employees. What was the problem with this organization? The problem was that the management was ineffective in leading teams and establishing a supportive environment that allows employees to feel safe and valued.

There is a difference between a manager and a leader; authority and accountability; and a successful organization and one that just is getting by. A business, a team, and an organization is only as good as its owners, coaches, and people in charge. Often, the employees get blamed for the failure of an organization, go through layoffs, hire days, and continue to keep the same management in place. I believe that is an awful way to assess your organizational structure. We must start at the top.

When my organization, Project SHINE, Inc., wasn't doing well, I would always put more work onto my team, give more tasks, and create new deadlines. The reality of it is was that I was doing a poor job leading and managing the tasks that were currently outlined. My team was doing an excellent job, I fell short, and it led to having to halt programs for the rest of one of our critical quarters. As a manager, you should learn how to effectively train and teach your team the steps and have them work with you —not for you. When you empower your employees and create a safe environment for your employees to thrive, they will not only run through a brick wall, but they will elevate you into delivering high-quality results. Learn to lead through effective delegation of responsibilities. Don't just tell people what to do. Hold your team accountable by teaching and training them how to do it. Delegation develops employee confidence, leadership, and work skills because they believe that you trust in their work.

In early 2016, I held a training workshop for early entrepreneurs in Huntsville, Alabama. I made a statement that sparked an in-depth conversation during class. I said, "Your employees are not just numbers, they are people first." Stop being so focused on the numbers, bottom line, and data and take some time to focus on the person or persons standing right in front of you. Employees want to do a good job and feel valued within their work, so it is up to you to create that environment. Recognize their achievements and reward them for doing a job well done.

The best way to recognize your employees' achievements is simply saying, "Thank you." As a professional, I can probably count on one hand the amount of times I've heard gratitude for the work I produced and the contribution I made. Hearing those two powerful words, "Thank you." is like hearing "I'm sorry." after someone has disappointed you, and all you wanted was a simple apology. It creates a peaceful environment that just makes you feel good inside. When you begin to set the tone and create a peaceful, safe environment, as a successful leader, you learn how to make an organization a place of fun and not just work.

Without a doubt, running a company is serious business, but it's hard to run your life as well, and you are getting by every day. Managing your goals, finances, and personal relationships is equivalent to managing corporate deadlines and strategies, stock valuation, and business relationships. The difference between your life and a company is that you are doing them all simultaneously, and an organization has different departments.

THE MISSION PLAN: THE DESTINY

Pull out your notebook or journal and answer the following questions.

1. Who does your inner circle consist of?
2. Who do you consider a mentor or coach?
3. Are there people in your life that no longer serve a purpose?
4. What type of support do you lack?
5. Who can you reach out to for this support?

TIPS FOR SUCCESS

A great mentor is not selfish; they are selfless and remember how they were when they were just starting in their careers.

The only way to keep yourself and your locker room of love from quitting on the mission is to take retreat off the table.

Hold your team accountable by teaching and training them how to do it.

"The essence of strategy is choosing what NOT to do."
— Michael Porter

CHAPTER ONE
POURING FROM AN EMPTY GLASS

When I graduated college with a degree in finance, I had a plethora of opportunities to choose from. The various companies that showed interest all wanted to provide me with an entry-level foundation to prove myself a potential leader in the company. I worked for a year as a Pharmaceutical Sales Representative in the Dermatology franchise for Janssen Biotech, Inc., a Johnson and Johnson company.

At the time, Johnson & Johnson was the number one Healthcare Provider and a worldwide brand bringing in billions of dollars annually. They were the premier brand and a globally-recognized franchise. From the outside looking in, I was proud to be a part of a great organization. I was one of ten other students selected from around the country to be a part of the College Hire program and the only student brought on to represent a Historically Black College/University (HBCU).

The job was great, I had complete autonomy on my daily

THE MISSION PLAN: THE DESTINY

schedule, traveled the world, made great connections, had a company car, and made great money. It was an overall great experience. I learned so much in this profession, and it truly helped me become a stronger professional and a better man. It taught me the true power of building lasting and authentic relationships and how much that can influence life and drive business decisions. I learned the importance of consistency and that every day is another today to practice your skillset and become a true business professional. But the longer I stayed in the industry, the longer I became "The Drug Rep." Instead of the man who would stand out for who he was and how he could help people, I was just known as the man in the suit with samples; not a man on a mission.

I wanted to be more than someone who created value for the moment; I pondered how I could provide value long term. At first, I came into the company to help patients, but the more I realized that I was helping a company, and that the drugs were helping patients, the more I realized how much I was replaceable and not truly valued. I grew to hate being just another and I wanted to be the one. I didn't want to settle to be just something, I wanted to be it.

Many times, we think we are irreplaceable until we get replaced. We forget the importance of constantly building our skillsets, perfecting our craft, and sharpening our strengths. The message here is that your job on earth is worth more than a salary. Your job on earth is worth more than the numbers on that paystub every two weeks. You are worth more than that life insurance policy, investment portfolio, 401K, or that pension plan that you are preparing for your children. You are worth more than that house you live in, that luxury car you drive, or even those clothes that wrap around your closet. Your assignment here on earth is deeper than a paper you have to turn into your professor. It is more meaningful than the test scores. Your life is more important than how many followers you have on social media, or how many people clap and yell at your graduation. That decision to invest in that company has no comparison to the true return when you choose to invest in the fellow man or woman standing next to you, in front of you, or behind you.

It is always said that the investment in ourselves is the greatest investment we could ever make in life. I truly believe the greatest investment is the resources, time, and energy that we give to other people and the seeds that we plant into the world. When it rains, it doesn't just rain on you; it rains on everyone. The difference is the covering, the jacket, the umbrellas, and the different levels of protection people have from the storm. What type of person can watch someone running or walking in the rain while they remain under their umbrella dry? It is not the principle of sharing everything; it is the principle of character and supporting everyone. The steps that you take moving forward into your life are all part of the steps that help you understand your true mission, your true purpose, and your true destiny. Like the steps when companies hire new talent, when companies open new offices or even move their headquarters, or even when companies decide to take their companies public. When private companies decide to take their companies public to sell shares on the New York Stock Exchange, there are many regulations, factors, and steps that need to be taken for that to be a successful completion. When we choose to make ourselves public and

THE MISSION PLAN: THE DESTINY

invest in the future of humanity, all it takes is a leap of faith and the approval of only yourself.

The experiences, trials and tribulations, obstacles that we overcome, weaknesses that we strengthened, and even the people that we helped along the way, all are factors of our stock rising and increasing the value in our lives. There are many factors during stock trading that lead to the valuation of a company or a stock price, however, in life, the things we go through are the factors that add value and increase our ability to inflict change on other people. Jim Rohn quoted, "Motivation is what gets you started. Habit is what keeps you going." In a recent article published in Success Magazine, "Rohn: How to Make Yourself More Valuable," Jim Rohn stated that labor combined with skills produces miracles. We always talk about giving back, helping others, investing energy, time, and resources into others so you can plant seeds into the world. It is very hard to water the problems of the world when you have never taken the time to fill your bucket with the nutrients that could provide solutions. You can't pour from an empty glass, you cannot plant from an empty basket, and you sure cannot teach on topics that you do not possess the knowledge. You cannot ignite change if your ignorant of the actual problem that is creating the conflict. The definition of ignorance is a lack of knowledge or information. Albert Einstein, in the 18th century, stated, "Peace cannot be kept by force; it can only be achieved by understanding." We cannot force innovation by being ignorant; innovation comes by understanding, being familiar, obtaining knowledge, and educating your mind on not being forceful, but the forces inflicting innovation.

10 STEPS TO BEING GREAT
1. Be Happy
2. Eliminate the word "Can't"
3. Invest in a Coach, Trainer, or Mentor
4. Nurture Your Talents and Gifts
5. Goal Setting
6. Generate Confidence
7. Read Books
8. Empower Your Creativity
9. Attend Seminars and Workshops
10. Take Care of Your Health

Be Happy

Abraham Lincoln quoted, "Most people are about as happy as they make up their minds to be." Happiness starts with you. Every morning you wake up, every night before you go to bed, and during your day, happiness is a choice. You have control over your happiness and joy. Do not become a hostage to your environment, circumstances, or situations. Continue to be grateful for what you have while planning for what you want. Make negative situations positive and positive situations perfect. You have the power!

Eliminate the Word "CAN'T"

Whenever you say that you can't do something, you instantly put limitations on your success and a leash on your potential. Eliminating the word can't is a simple way to achieving massive success in your life. The cliché, "You can do anything you put your mind to," is real. Successful people aren't just good at what they do; they are great at saying yes when everyone said no. They are resilient and continue to believe in the power of change and opportunity.

Eliminate THESE Phrases
    "It won't work."
    "I can't afford it."
    "It doesn't happen like that."
    "I can't find it."
    "I can't do that."

Add THESE Phrases
    "I will."
    "I will find the money."
    "It will work out."
    "I CAN do this."
    "I will not be broken by this."
    "This is all part of the journey. I will be successful."
    "I just have to keep pushing."

Invest in a Coach, Trainer, or Mentor

    We talked about the power of mentorship earlier in the book, and I want to revisit that point because of the importance of investing in a coach, trainer, or mentor. Coaches are the assistance to your success strategies, the partner in your business, or life success, and it is their job to aid you in implementing your success plan. On CNN, I remember them stating that "coaching is the universal language of change and learning." It may not always cost money, but use your time and energy to invest in a coach, trainer, or mentor to develop your full potential.

Nurture Your Talents and Gifts

When you begin to invest in yourself, that world of opportunity will become accessible for you, and you will soon gain access. Your mind is the key card that gains you access, and it starts by nurturing your talents and gifts. What happens to a garden that you never water, and that never gets sunlight? It dies… If you are not adding water and sunlight to the crops of your life, then they will soon die. Get rid of the weeds in your life, and begin to nurture your talents and gifts.

Goal Setting

The moment you stop setting goals is the moment you become blind to your destination. It is like driving down a dark road at night without your headlights on or walking through your house without the lights on. If you don't know the direction you are going, you are destined to crash into something. Turn the light on and begin to set personal and business goals for yourself. As discussed in the previous book, your goals should be SMART – Specific, Measurable, Attainable, Relevant, and Timely.

Generate Confidence

Have you ever been somewhere and only a few people are responsible for creating the energy in the room? People seem to flock to and want to get to know those individuals. Those are the confident ones. People who know their worth and value, have something to say, and people want to listen. Generate and invest in your confidence by first developing an understanding of who you are and what you must offer to the world. Have courage in your character and speak truth and authenticity. The more you learn about yourself, the more confident you'll become in sharing it with others. By being vulnerable and open with others, this will, in turn, create great lasting relationships. Invest in generate that confidence by first learning yourself.

Read Books

Whether it is Dr. Seuss, Harry Potter, Machiavelli, or Socrates, reading is nothing but a resource to build your knowledge and expertise in any area. If you complain about time, read a chapter a day for 30 – 45 minutes. By the end of the year, you will have read 365 chapters of knowledge that you could add to your business, your ideas, and your life. Staying consistent and learning about different topics, cultures, or even ways that people overcame failure will provide you with a strong foundation as you plant your seeds in the ground of success. As Dr. Seuss stated himself, "The more you read, the more things you know. The more that you learn, the more places you'll go."

Empower Your Creativity

Empowering and investing in your creativity is important. Creativity is the catalyst in manifesting lifelong learning and activity. It is what we are known for and allows us to inspire or even be inspired, to have fun or pave our futures. The most beautiful thing about life is diversity, and that all starts by way of creativity and seeing life through different viewpoints. Take the time to empower your creativity by putting all those thoughts into action. Write your ideas down on paper daily, journal for 30 minutes to an hour a day. Draw that painting in your head, or say that poem that you can't stop thinking about. Bring your creative mind to life.

Attend Seminars and Workshops

Attending a seminar or various workshops has numerous benefits including networking with other professionals, increasing confidence, improving communication skills, or skills, strategies, or topics that add to your toolbox of skills. You will have the opportunity to have face to face interactions with different people who are motivated just like you are and get the opportunity to have your questions answered by like-minded people.

Take Care of Your Health

I recently read a book by Deepak Chopra and Rudolph E. Tanzi called Super Genes: Unlock the Astonishing Power of YOUR DNA for Optimum Health and Well-Being. It hit the mark on the importance of taking care of your health. In the book, there is a quote stating, "Lifestyle is the domain where transformation takes place." The book explains ways to add years to your life by altering your lifestyle into something healthy and filled with happiness. It explains how your genes react to experiences and how you react in your daily lives can essentially make a lasting impression in your overall life. Taking care of your health always starts with your diet and follows with activity/exercise. Your body is your Bentley, your luxury house, and the temple. You must fuel your body with the right nutrients to tackle those tough problems and conquer those amazing opportunities.

BEING OBLIVIOUSLY INSANE

Have you ever wondered why you do certain things? Have you ever thought why you hang out, spend time, or give attention to certain people? Or, even better, have you ever wondered why you aren't successful even though you are working hard, giving it all you've got, or spending a lot of money on your dreams? If you took genuinely focused time to think about those questions, you would find a correlation between the first two and why you are not successful. I call this mindset, "Being Obliviously Insane."

We are familiar with the word insanity or insane, so now, let's break down oblivious. The definition of oblivious is when you are not aware of or not concerned about what is happening around you. So being obliviously insane is when you are not aware of or not concerned about what is happening around you, continuing to do the same thing repeatedly and expecting different results. Once we break it down like this, does this sound like you or even people you may hang out with or know? You're oblivious that you keep following the same cycles, the same patterns, doing the same things, and getting the same results. You keep complaining about your situation, circumstance, or position, but you do not provide a solution to the actual problems. The true magic in life happens outside your comfort zone. Jillian Michaels said it best when she stated that you must "get comfortable with being uncomfortable." You must do things that make you uncomfortable, learn how to be flexible, and adapt to these new forms of doing things. You must do things that make you itch and scratch because you're not used to the feeling. Once the irritation is over, you typically find a breakthrough. In health, an itch means an outbreak or an allergic reaction. In life, that itchy feeling is an opportunity or realization of your potential. Don't ignore the itch and begin to treat yourself by performing surgery on old habits, useless relationships, and meaningless places. Stop being obliviously insane and become aware of the amazing opportunities available to you once you become comfortable being uncomfortable.

THE SUNGLASS EFFECT

Are you familiar with the benefits of the sun that wakes us up every morning? Do you know the true importance the sun has in our lives? According to Lynda Lampert in her article, "Six Important Things the Sun Does for You," she states that the sun is such a constant, reliable sight that few of us rarely acknowledge its existence. She continues during her article and explains that the sun is the primary reason life exists on earth. She believes that the most important things the sun does for you are:

1. Food Energy
2. Vitamin D
3. Happiness
4. Warmth
5. Light
6. Precipitation

When I initially read this article, I didn't know all the benefits of the sun because I never took the time to acknowledge it. I expected it to rise every morning, and always be there. I never took the time to understand it or what would happen if it wasn't there. Even so, I would wear sunglasses during the day to block my eyes from the sun rays. I used sunblock to protect my skin and got the windows of my car tinted to protect me from the sun. After reading this article, I noticed that I was hiding from the sun instead of embracing it. I was doing everything to stay away from it instead of appreciating its very existence.

How many times in your life have you pondered on what you are trying to hide from? How many times have you embraced the inner light within you? How many times have you acknowledged your strengths and true gifts that make you, you? Are you hiding behind those clothes or in that car with those tinted windows? Do you remember the dreams you had and people distracted you or blocked you from the success or sunlight of opportunity? Do you remember what you did? Did you put on another shade of distraction, or did you begin to acknowledge the sunlight of opportunity? Every day, we give attention to things that don't deserve our time, people who don't deserve our acknowledgment, and situations that don't deserve our energy. When we look at success, it's like the light at the end of the tunnel, and everything that you let in that path of the sunlight begins to dim your dream. Eventually, you will no longer see what you want and be barricaded by the non-believers, the haters, or the attention snatchers. It is time for you to stop adding shades to your success and begin to see through the lens of your destiny.

ONE PIN FROM PERFECTION

"Strike Nine! Yes! Just one more to go." She says after bowling her ninth straight strike in a row during the bowling competition. In bowling games that use ten pins, such as ten-pin bowling, the highest possible score is 300, achieved by bowling 12 strikes in a row in a single game: one strike in each of the first nine frames, and three more in the tenth frame.

She had already bowled nine consecutive strikes, and now she began to feel the pressure going into the tenth frame. As she walked over to get her ball off the rack, she looks around, and to her, it felt like the world had stopped, and all eyes were on her. No balls were being rolled in the individual lanes; there was no noise or chatter from the crowd. All eyes and attention were on the possibility of her rolling the tenth strike, and the fans witnessing a potential perfect score. According to Cliff Schrock in his article, "Records & Rarities: The unlikely ace/300 game double," "It's a 3,000 to 1 chance for a tour player and a 5,000 to 1 chance for a low-handicapper player to roll a perfect game. Similar to making an ace, the more proficient you are at bowling, the better your chance of a 300 game. The odds for a PBA bowler rolling a 300 are 460 to 1, while it is 11,500 to 1 for the average bowler."

During this time, the crowd was witnessing close to the impossible, and the odds were not in her favor. As she walked down to the lane, she prepared her footing, took a deep breath, and let the bowl out of her hand. The crowd froze, the music paused, and the girl closed her eyes. As the ball met the pins, we witnessed what once seemed a high possibility become an instant disappointment as one pin was left standing as the ball went to be racked. As the girl walked away from her lane, the music played loudly, the crowd was unfrozen, and the once cheers of excitement became the chatter of disbelief. The girl instantly said to her teammate, "I knew when the ball left my hand, that it wasn't going to be a strike. My fingers were in the wrong place, and I rushed it." With body language of sadness and grief, the girl, days, months, and years later, never forgot the feeling she felt from being one pin away from perfection. How many times in our lives do we look back and regret a decision we made, an opportunity that we missed, or even a time where we just missed the mark? How did that one time shape the course of the rest of your life? What if that one experience ended in your favor? What feeling would you have gotten? How would it have changed your life? We cannot let our problems or lack of preparation affect us from the true possibility of perfection. We cannot let those minor details hold us back from the perfect score of success. It is the smallest things that have the biggest impact on our lives. The routines, bad habits, lack of commitment, procrastination, or gossiping have a long-term effect on our performance, efficiency, and lives. Persistent preparation prepares us for times of pressure and opens the door of opportunity and excellence.

THE MISSION PLAN: THE DESTINY

Pull out your notebook or journal and answer the following questions.

1. Re-read the 10 Steps to Become Great.
2. Write each step in your journal.
3. Beside each step, write ways you can begin to apply or act on each step.

TIPS FOR SUCCESS

The greatest investment is the resources, time, and energy that we give to other people and the seeds that we plant into the world.

You cannot ignite change if your ignorant of the actual problem that is creating the conflict.

You must do things that make you uncomfortable, learn how to be flexible, and adapt to these new forms of doing things.

CHAPTER TWO
EIGHT ROUNDS OF SUCCESS

It was October 30, 1974, and the sky was lit by the stars and prayers of the thousands of fans attending what some said was the best World Heavyweight Championship of all time. The venue was set at the 20th of May Stadium in Kinshasa, Zaire and the contenders were the great George Foreman vs. The one and only Muhammad Ali. It is said that Ali is famed for his speed and technical skills, whereas Foreman's raw power was his greatest strength. George Foreman led every round by power punches. Ali never backed down, although he continued to take hit after hit. It wasn't until the eighth round that the voices of the fight commentators were all that lit the radio ways around the world...

"Left hand thrown out by Foreman. The humidity here is about 85-90—24-year-old Foreman hanging pretty tough in there. I caution you to look for the one-punch knockout from George Foreman at any time. This guy is devastating, to say the least, and can take you out at any particular time. Foreman tried to throw a sneaky right hand at Ali. Ali is hanging on here; he is getting away with it, getting away with it. The punches can take punches, and they will not hurt Ali. Foreman has thrown a lot of punches now; maybe this is the tactic of Ali. Here we go. Ali a sneaky right hand; another sneaky right hand. Now he is working over the shoulder; there goes a combination. Down goes Foreman. Down goes Foreman. 5…6…7…8…9… Ali has done it again; the Greatest has done the unthinkable. This is the most joyous scene ever seen in the history of boxing. Muhammad Ali has won! Muhammad Ali has won! By a knockout, by a knockout…The greatest fight in boxing history!"

Losers get knocked down because winners get back up. In our lives, we have choices in every decision and action we make. We can choose to wake up in the morning on the first alarm or choose to hit the snooze button and maybe get to work late. We can choose to finish that assignment early and plan for any contingencies, or wait until the last minute and turn in something lacking quality. When we get knocked down in life, we can choose to get up and keep moving forward or stay there, complain and settle for mediocrity. Life isn't problem proof, and getting knocked down is a part of life. However, it is what we choose that makes the difference in our success or failure. Skill doesn't win games. Power doesn't win championships. Talent doesn't break records. Preparation and resilience are the keys that unlock the door of success and set the foundation for a lifelong legacy. It may take four games, four quarters, or even eight rounds, however, it is those who continue to take hit after hit, sack after sack, loss after loss during the regular season, who will eventually come out as the champions in the last minute, quarter or round.

    The world witnessed one of the greatest second-half comebacks in NFL history in Super Bowl 51 between the Atlanta Falcons and the New England Patriots. It was their second Super Bowl appearance in 51 years of existence. The world was convinced this game was over at halftime. The Falcons led 21-0 late in the second quarter and ended up going into halftime with 21 and the Patriots with three from a late second-quarter field goal. The most beautiful thing about life, just like sports, is that it is not over until it is over. Tom Brady rallied his team and marched New England down the field again and again, stunning the Patriots in this epic comeback scoring 31 unanswered points to win their fifth Super Bowl. Tom Brady threw 466 passing yards, which is the most ever in Super Bowl history. He overcame the largest deficit in Super Bowl history playing in the first overtime game in Super Bowl history. Your setback in life is the very platform for your comeback. The first and second quarter deficits you face are preparing you for halftime and to have the greatest comeback of history. You are preparing to rally and march down the field again and again and again, stunning the people that didn't believe in you, stunning the friends that didn't support you, or the ones that put limits on your potential. It is never too late in the game to make a comeback, but it starts with you continuing to remember the mission at hand and believe in yourself, your talents, and that you have enough time to manage in the second half of life.

IF...

After invading southern Greece and receiving the submission of other key city-states, Philip II of Macedon sent a message to Sparta saying, "You are advised to submit without further delay, for if I bring my army on your land, I will destroy your farms, slay your people and raze your city."

Sparta replied, "If." Subsequently, neither Philip nor his son Alexander the Great attempted to capture the city. As the Spartans did in the Greek World, you must have prowess in battling your tribulations, trials, enemies, and overcoming those obstacles with actions and not words. The Spartan Army was trained in the discipline and honor of the warrior society. The Spartan Army was the lifeline and blood that flowed through the Spartan City State. Even though Thebes defeated Sparta in the Battle of Leuctra in 371 BC ending their prominent role in Greece, the mindset and Spartan Mentality live forever. The way of not backing down to obstacles and overcoming them by never laying down the weapon of your mind "for any reason, be it hunger or danger." Like the Spartans being the most feared military forces in the Greek World, the unknown heights of your mind fear those who don't understand your potential. Conquer your enemies by elevating your mind and unlocking your potential. When people doubt your potential respond with "If..."

THE JOURNEY OF AN ENTREPRENEUR

Most people only pay attention to the final product of a successful entrepreneur. These same people usually say things like, "They got lucky, or I can't be like them..." But what most don't see is what they overcome: the daily struggles, rejections, rumors, heartaches, criticisms, and empty bank accounts. All those lonely nights trying to make a dream a reality, and even the friends lost on the way trying to chase a dream. Sometimes life is about risking everything for a dream no one can see but you. The only difference between the one who made it and the one who didn't isn't the resources. It isn't an opportunity. It isn't the timing. It is the mindset. The people who made it outworked everyone, hustled every day, appreciated the daily grind, accepted the mentorship, and was coachable to receive the knowledge they learned every day. The only difference between the one who made it and the one who didn't is every day they felt like quitting, but every day they kept working, and through those hardships, they became successful. Money is a result. Wealth is a result. Health is a result. Illness is a result. Weight is a result. The only way to change the outer results of our actions, we must change our inner worlds by building better habits.

After college, I was interviewing for a position with Stryker Corporation, at the time, the world's leader in Medical Device Technology. One of the questions I was asked was, "Kyle, what tempo do you like to work? Do you like to be productive in spurts, or do you like to be a steady paced worker?" When my father used to coach me in sports, he always used to tell his athletes to "be quick, but not in a hurry." Back then, it never resonated with me until I was asked this question in a professional setting. It's okay to be quick to get to a result, but not in a hurry where you miss critical steps that could cost you more damage financially or even your career. You can desire to get somewhere quick, but you must trust and appreciate the process. We can't be such in a rush that we are ungrateful or unaware of the steps we miss.

As an entrepreneur, it is about the constant focus and steadily productive work and not about riding on a career or corporate roller coaster. It is not about having a strong Monday or Tuesday of solid work and beginning to fall on Wednesday and Thursday, and by the weekend, you don't have enough motivation or willpower to keep pushing forward.

In the 2016 NBA season, the Golden State Warriors made NBA history. They were victorious in the regular season but lost in a devastating game seven after being up 3-1 in the championship series. Life isn't about the regular season; it is about preparing ourselves for the playoffs and staying consistent to win the final match and overcome those final obstacles. Have you ever seen people that do not do any work during the regular season, workweek, or regular day but when it is playoff time, end of the quarter, or end of the year, they begin to work hard? When people see the incentives of potential bonuses or want to get a positive performance review, they begin to work hard those last few months or weeks to make a good impression? As an entrepreneur, you must keep that success and dream you have set as the ultimate incentive every day. You must give your performance reviews; you must be your boss and board of directors. You must assess your performance every day and don't lose sight of your work.

During my tenure with Johnson & Johnson, one of my colleagues would say, "In the workplace, you must work to work every day like you are a landlord and rent is due every day." I remember him describing it to the point where I began to live my life as such. You should be accomplishing tasks every day. Never become bored because if you are bored, that means you are wasting and losing time to solve that problem you set out to solve or even accomplish tasks you said you would accomplish. If you are persistent, you will get it. If you are consistent, you will keep it. Continue to stay committed to change, growth, and development. Spoil yourself with consistency, and you will begin to witness the shift in the atmosphere.

LIFE TIME WAR

It was February 8, 2017, and I was without a job, without a car, without any savings, and my bank account was overdrawn $452.00. I had a trip planned the same weekend to go to Cancun, Mexico. I had $200 in cash in my wallet, and I was about $18k in debt. I sat for hours trying to figure out a way to capitalize on that $200, make a $200 investment and turn it into a $200K return or a 2M dollar wealth opportunity. Some of you sitting reading this are probably in the same predicament or even worse. Some of you may owe money, not have assets, are overwhelmed with liabilities, and don't know your next move. Many of you want success and wealth so badly that you have been the very reason you don't have it. You are so caught up in the big ideas, the large investment return opportunities, and the "game-changers," where sometimes, it is the smallest and most simple ideas that produce those game-changer financial opportunities. At times, it is that procedure, service, or product you always complain about or always have suggestions for that maybe be your gold mine and opportunity to create a solution.

Do you think success comes easy? Do you think wealth and happiness, peace, and joy are something we just wake up with and can easily do every day? Life is a lifetime war, and every day you wake up, every challenge, every obstacle, every trial, and tribulation you face is a battle. You will win and lose some battles, but the goal should always be to win the war. The goal should always be to come out on top at the end of the sacrifices, lessons, hardships, pain, and bloodshed. You're the only opponent and enemy that you are fighting. You are battling the fight to be accepted, successful in terms of society, wanted, and loved by your spouse, respected by your children and cohorts. You are battling the fight of not getting the promotion at work even though you were overqualified or not getting your insurance company to cover you after that accident, even if though it wasn't your fault. Some people will continue to bash you down into the dirt when times are tough. Some people will continue to keep a scorecard of your wrongs instead of giving you praise for your positive achievements. Some people will even keep a scorecard of what they have done for you and use that against you. Never take no for an answer. Go after your biggest dream and never settle; because you can be anything that you want to be in life if you are willing to fight.

INCREASING HUMAN CAPACITY

Whether you're an executive, a rising entrepreneur, or a student trying to find your lane, have you ever wondered what it would be like to have a twin? Have you ever wondered what it would be like if you had two of you when working on those tasks, handling those projects, or even inspiring those communities? What would you give to have a clone? How productive could you be? How much time could you save? How many opportunities could you create for others if you just had someone that went as hard as you? This is when you must learn how to increase your capacity and understand how to multiply what you're doing. This happens in many startup companies. They have just outgrown their market that their offices are in, and they are trying to figure out the next steps. Often, in these board meetings, they suggest a different product line, a different clientele, and throw money into more marketing. Those three things will lead to a decline in revenue and will end up diminishing the brand. An effective way to increase capacity, whether for your brand or your organization, is to expand to other areas and markets. That has been the power and result of the online market featuring e-commerce because organizations then have no bounds, and they can sell their products to anyone in the world. You don't have to walk into stores in that one city; you can download the company app or go to the company's website and get the product that everyone has been talking about.

Capacity is about working not externally but on your company's ability to do more internally, such as speeding up production or improving your systems and processes. The same goes for your brand. It is not always about throwing products in different markets. It is sometimes about learning how you can fill a need for a specific customer base in a potential marketplace. To be successful in business, the bottom line is that you have to look beyond the transaction. Successful companies have figured out the methodology behind the importance of person-to-person experience by having valuable conversations that spark and create curiosity. People, your customers, and clients do not buy what you have or what you do; they buy why you are doing it. The word "why" isn't external. This is an internal value or fundamental purpose of doing what you are doing, selling what you are selling, and proposing what you are proposing.

In an organization, you have to learn the power of communicating from inside out. To create a product for a targeted customer, you must begin with the purpose, followed by a unique process and innovation. Apple Inc. is not just successful because they have amazingly innovative products. They have found a way to align their core organizational belief systems by being a "different kind of company with a different view of the world," and building a team of believers and not just skilled workers.

When someone is skilled, they will do a good job; when someone believes in what they are doing, they will create value for the company. Steve Jobs quoted, "Marketing is about values. It's a complicated and noisy world, and we're not going to get a chance to get people to remember much about us. No company is. So, we have to be clear about what we want them to know about us."

Before we can create value for that organization, community, and world, we must like the picture that we are painting. Warren Buffet quoted, "It is hard to paint a picture that you don't want to look at. You have to paint your own masterpiece." You are the painter on your canvas of life. To complete your masterpiece, you must know who you are, where you are going, and what brand you want to communicate. How well you do, the job has very little to do with how successful you are in your professional career. Or even further, how well you perform only accounts for about 10% of your overall success. Harvey Coleman, in his book, Empowering Yourself, The Organizational Game Revealed, briefly states that there are three elements to career success: performance, image, and exposure.

As stated briefly, performance only accounts for about 10% of your overall success. This is about you, the day to day work that you are tasked with, and the overall quality of the results you deliver. This is simply about how well you do what you do. Image is different and accounts for about 30% of your overall career success. This is about your brand and what other people think about you. Are you the solutionist or the problematic road blocker that always highlights the issues and never offers a valuable way of tackling it? To say it simply, this is the impression that you make on others and how people view you as an individual and professional. Exposure carries the bulk and, according to Coleman, accounts for about 60% of your overall career success. If you are self-employed, then these weights may need to be adjusted, but exposure is about who knows about you, what you do, and how well you are performing. Do your managers and their managers know about you and how you are always delivering results? Does your team just know you, or do other people outside of your department, organization, and region know who you are and what you do? This is critical, and it is truly important for career success. Now this book was written in the 1960s and may use different language, so today we call it, "it is not about what you know, it is about who you know and who knows you." Stuart Britt quoted, "Doing business without advertising is like winking at a girl in the dark. You know what you are doing, but nobody else does." A business or life without exposure is like living in the dark. You have to shine light on what you do, but you have to make sure others are aware of where the light is shining.

Pull out your notebook or journal and answer the following questions.

1. Create a timeline of your journey to where you are today. Be sure to include successes, failures, and breakthroughs.

2. Review your journey and ask yourself the following questions.

- Would you be where you are today without the failures you experienced?
- How have you changed?
- How do you hope the rest of your journey to success spans out?

THE MISSION PLAN: THE DESTINY

TIPS FOR SUCCESS

Talent doesn't break records. Preparation and resilience are the keys that unlock the door of success and set the foundation for a lifelong legacy.

It is never too late in the game to make a comeback, but it starts with you continuing to remember the mission at hand and believe in yourself, your talents, and that you have enough time to manage in the second half of life.

CHAPTER THREE
THE GOLD MEDALIST OF LIFE

It was always my dream to attend college and receive a scholarship to play Division One sports. When I was privileged to attend Alabama A&M University on a full-ride track and field scholarship, I remember the feeling that went through my veins the first day I came to campus. I remember pulling up with my parents in our XC90 Volvo, hearing the band play, seeing how welcoming the people were, and smelling the freshly prepared food from the cafeteria that I would soon fall in love with in the coming months. I can recall the smell of fresh-cut grass and how beautiful the landscaping was around the campus. I watched other students interact with their parents and noticed how proud each parent looked. As I took in the campus, I realized that my dreams had come true.

I've long since moved on from my college days, however, I have never forgotten how it felt when I arrived at Alabama A&M. When I set goals for myself, I think about how it will feel once I achieve them. I visualize what I want. I think about what my dream home will smell like when I walk into it. I imagine what it will feel like to fly in a private jet that I own. I see myself wearing the tailor-made suits I desire. I also keep in mind what success looks like to me. Very often, we feel like we aren't successful because of other people's definitions of success. It looks different for every individual. My success looks like educational programs and schools built globally to empower the next generation of future business leaders and groom them to be excellent professionals. My memories help me realize the work needed to obtain those monuments of success.

In college, I ran the 200 and 400-meter dashes; I was a sprinter. It was a lot different for me because I was accustomed to running a mile or even two miles and only kicking up the speed at the end. Now, I had to learn how to get comfortable being uncomfortable. So many of you are used to doing what you have been doing for a long time. You are used to having the same daily schedules, hanging out with the same people, making the same decisions, and living the same mediocre lives that you complain about. When you get comfortable being uncomfortable, you learn to adapt and grow in other areas of your life. A good friend of mine, a meditation and therapy guru, once said to me that you cannot heal the body until you heal all parts of the mind. It resonated with me so much because I know many people with million-dollar dreams and welfare work ethic. You may want a Bentley, but the amount of time you have invested in your dream will only yield a Nissan Versa.

To be successful in track, preparation is key. Paying attention to the smallest, minute details allows runners to increase their skills in distance and strength. Your leg form, the degree of your arms, the equipment you use during training, and even the spikes you run with during competitions determine your success as a runner. The best runners have unique workouts that help them improve their endurance and speed. Using special techniques like running up hills, jumping in sand, or being pulled back by a parachute as you are running at your full speed down a football field improve your performance during track meets and competitions. No matter where a runner starts, only the most prepared, best trained, and most focused track runners receive gold medals at the Summer Olympics.

15 STEPS TO BECOME A GOLD MEDALIST OF LIFE

#1 Finding Your Stride | What's Your Passion?

When I ran track, they taught us to find our stride. I remember coming around that curve in the 400-meter race, trying to find that kick to finish the race, and my coach would yell from the stands, "Find your stride! Stride into the finish line!" In track, we call it finding your stride, but in life, we can call it finding your lane. In life, we must find our passion. We must find what makes us tick. We must understand what keeps us up all night. We must pinpoint the things we find ourselves thinking about. We have to realize the topics that others hear us talking about all the time. Our passion is the fuel of our dreams. When we don't have that source, we find ourselves in the same place year after year.

In track, many people may want to be a 100-meter sprinter, but if you are most talented as a mile or 800-meter runner, you must find the right placement and perfect your craft. In earlier chapters, we discussed how to adapt and become comfortable being uncomfortable. However, it is also important to learn our natural gifts and what comes easy to us. Most of the time, the things that people polish and perfect cause them to become successful. Doing so allows us to find joy and fulfillment in what we do.

David Shands, entrepreneur, business coach, and author, wrote in his book, Dreams are Built Overnight, that he is not a motivational speaker. There is a difference between a motivational speaker such as Eric Thomas or Jeremy Anderson, two of the most popular and world-renowned speakers, versus someone like myself or David Shands. He went on to talk about staying in your lane, perfecting your craft, finding what works for you, and being the best at it. Just because someone may give you a title doesn't mean you are held to that title's constraints. You must find ways to separate your skills and gifts and make a name for yourself through authenticity.

#2 Optimize Your Cadence | Goals and Strategic Planning

In track, a key factor is your cadence, your steps per minute, or how fast you get to a particular point. When I was in school, a good professor/mentor named Dr. Smith, an author, and a very successful businessman, asked me, "Kyle, what is your optimization level?" He explained that my optimization level was ultimately everything that I wanted; the best possible outcome for my life. He then asked, "What is your balance level? What are the things that you actually need? Your optimization level is the top of the top, that salary, that location, that benefits package. But what do you actually need?" Optimizing your cadence is important because it helps you strategically set goals and plan for your life. When we realize and organize our priorities, we can understand how to align our passion with our priorities. So, optimize your cadence and set those goals. Make sure that you have daily, weekly, monthly, and yearly goals. Work within what you want to do, and do it with passion. Keep your priorities in mind and cut the fluff or unnecessary things. Optimize your cadence!

#3 Adjust Your Stride to The Terrain

Everyone has walked, ran, or done some type of physical activity at some point in their lives. How you do certain physical activities changes depending on the terrain or surface you're on. When you adjust to your terrain, you're not just changing your stride or optimizing to a different cadence. You are becoming adaptable and flexible to your terrain. I run differently when I'm on a track than when I'm on a street. When you're on a track, there is a little more bounce than running on the street. Sometimes it's good to try new terrains so you can learn how to be flexible.

The only thing constant in life is change, so as we begin to change our strategies, goals, success plans, and environment, we must understand how to adjust ourselves to the terrain. You can't expect to make a difference in yourself or the world if you can't adjust to the culture.

#4 Leverage Instruction

I give a lot of credit to my coaches. They have challenged me and taught me several things. One of the most vital lessons was how to change my form so I wouldn't have an injury. Sometimes, in track, you can be running the wrong way. Years ago, when I was running at a track meet, a runner broke her femur. I don't want to blame her or her coaches because things happen. However, this incident taught me that we must learn to leverage the instruction we receive from mentors so we can dodge pain, failure, or disappointment. We must posture ourselves to learn from these people and become servant leaders.

Many times, as entrepreneurs, business owners, and millennials, we are too quick to want to lead. After school, I had an opportunity to be an entrepreneur, but I needed to learn from the best of the best, so I went to work for Johnson and Johnson. I learned how to serve an organization, manager, and corporation. As I submitted myself as a student, I learned the laws of leadership. I was grateful for this opportunity because it gave me the lessons I needed before becoming an entrepreneur.

Understand that it's not always about what we think is best, what we learned, and what we want to change. We have to leverage the instruction. We have to learn from and gain mentors. Doing so allows us to learn from the mistakes of others instead of making those same mistakes. A quote states, "A fool learns from his own experiences, but a wise man learns from the experiences of others."

#5 Observe Experienced Runners| Be a Student of the Game

Everyone isn't going to make it to the top right away. The sweet taste of sweat during your preparation makes winning more rewarding. We can't be so focused on falling short that we don't analyze our mistakes. Sometimes, we must learn from the winner to become sharper and more prepared. It's important to observe winners and ask questions like, "What books were they reading? What strategies worked for them? What were their daily schedules? What types of associations were they a part of? Where did they spend most of their time?" When something goes wrong, we have a natural inclination to wonder where we could have done something differently, and how can we improve next time? Self-assessment is incredible, and that is one of the success tips that we will discuss later in this chapter. However, learning from those who won is the best remedy for understanding where we may fall short. As athletes, whether your sport is track and field, basketball, football, golf, soccer, baseball, or gymnastics, we are taught to study the greatest athletes. We are expected to watch films and videos, listen to interviews, learn the workouts, or just follow their diet plans. As a track and field athlete, if I didn't make it to the final championship round, I would sit in the stands alone and study the racers to become better, sharper, and more durable. I watched how they warmed up before the race, how they sat in the blocks, their form during the race, the intensity in their faces, and even their body language. We can't expect to have a wealth mindset when we are only giving it a penny's worth of knowledge or attention. We can't expect to be amongst the game changers and the playmakers if we are always learning from procrastinators. We must become what we see as success.

#6 Go with What You Feel | Follow Your Gut

Our instruction or mentorship will often try to steer us left or right. Sometimes, we must follow our gut feeling and stick to it. Believers call a spirit of discernment or the promptings of the Holy Spirit. It is an intuitive feeling that burns in us. At times, this feeling may be in alignment with the wisdom of our mentors or coaches. At those rare moments when it doesn't, we must do what's best for us.

#7 Have Good Posture | Body Language

Body language is the key to effective communication. Very often, non-verbal ques outweighs the language we use. One of the first key things people notice is someone's posture, how they present, and carry themselves. Is their back straight up? Are they walking tall with their chest out and their head up? Do they look you in your eyes when you speak? Do they give you a firm handshake as an introduction? Body language is essential. It sets the tone before you even open your mouth. Many people discern your intentions from your body language rather than what you actually articulate. In track and field, the smallest details make or break a runner and set the gold medalists apart from the runners-up. So, what's your body language communicating? Are you focused? Are you investing enough time in your dreams and passions? Are you having the right conversations? Are you asking the right questions? The smallest things can make the most significant impact on our lives.

#8 Control Your Breathing | Relax

Take 20 seconds to close your eyes and breath. Take three deep breaths in and out. As you close your eyes, think of all that you want to accomplish and let that be the center of your focus.

There is so much power in taking deep breaths. Have you ever noticed that when you are stressing, disappointed, afraid, anxious, or excited, your breathing becomes quick, shallow, and choppy? The key to controlling your emotions is breathing fully, slowly, and deeply. When you are emotionally overwhelmed, take 20-30 seconds to breathe. Close your eyes and visualize what you are working towards. Put your dreams or goals at the center of your mind, relax, and breathe. As you breathe out, release any feelings of doubt, disappointment, and frustration. Remind yourself that this is all apart of the process, and your current situation is a learning opportunity. Encourage yourself by imagining how it will feel to make it to the other side of preparation. Control your feelings. Control your breathing. Control your success.

#9 Dress for Success

Dress for the occasion and not for the situation. A clean and neat professional appearance is vital when trying to make a good first impression. It sends a message to others that you are professional. Stacia Pierce from the Huffington Post wrote in a journal entry, "What Does It Mean to Dress for Success," "A keen sense of style when it comes to your image can lead to greater opportunities and higher levels of success. Dress for the role you want, not the role you have." You can't run a great race in track if you have football cleats. You can't show up to a basketball game with a helmet. You can't be ready to excel in life without the proper equipment. Showing up to your company's investment meeting without the company's profile is the same as showing up to an interview without your resume. It's like showing up to class without paper and a writing utensil on test day. We must understand that every day is test day, and our position in life is the determining score that we get on the daily quizzes, the monthly tests, and quarterly personal exam reviews. We are tested every day to see if we will work hard or procrastinate, perform or watch from the sidelines, win or lose. But it isn't always about physically dressing for success. We must also ensure that we are mentally dressed for success.

#10 Stretch

Many runners seldom stretch after a race — I know I didn't. I always wondered why I couldn't break my records or experienced soreness the day after a race. Have you ever thought that you were working so hard at something, doing things so flawlessly, but you still couldn't get to the next level? Or, no matter how hard you tried, you couldn't break that bad habit? Or, get away from that person? You must learn the power of stretching after certain checkpoints in your life. Stretching is equivalent to assessing yourself. You have to have an assessment period and begin to set timelines on your work. Set a time frame to work on something. At the end of that time frame, assess what you need to adjust or work on more. Don't wait until the end of something to figure out how to solve a problem. Allow yourself to assess and make adjustments before the deadline.

Failing to schedule moments of assessment causes us to waste time and get behind on our goals. Begin to assess your progress, set timelines, stick to deadlines, and empower your entrepreneurial spirit to learn how to begin to stretch when you are finished. Stop wasting your time and resources on habitual habits and trust the process of assessing progress.

#11 Adjust Expectations | Set Higher Standards

After you assess yourself, adjust your expectations, and create higher standards. The creation of new goals, innovation of new thoughts, and implementation of new processes allow you to move beyond mediocrity and into excellence.

#12 Stick to the Schedule | Commitment

Abraham Lincoln once said, "Commitment is what transforms a promise into a reality." Motivation is what you need to get started, but commitment keeps you going. Commitment requires us to have the courage to keep going after a mistake, the strength to fight through after weaknesses are exposed, and the passion to perform through the tough transformation process. Over a period, you will begin to run faster, longer, and stronger. We can't expect quick results. Success is a process and lifestyle of small steps of hard work that position us to finish strong. Imagine if you worked on your dream for an hour a day for a whole year. By the end of the year, you would have put 365 hours into your dream.

Some studies show that it takes 10,000 hours to become a professional expert at something. Put in the hours in now so you can reap the benefits later. Achieving success is like gardening. You have to do more than plant seeds. You must nurture, water, and ensure they receive the right amount of sunlight. If you fail to do so, the seed remains a seed. However, if you take the time to care for it, it will bloom into something you can benefit from. Aren't you tired of being a seed and just having potential? Aren't you ready to become? Start watering your goals, nurturing and putting time into your dreams, and shining light on your weaknesses. I don't know about you, but I'd rather have a solid success than an overnight failure. Trust the process because it will be worth it in the end.

#13 Execute

A business plan is nothing but words on paper. It means nothing until you start executing it. What you thought would work will change once it has been applied, and you can see the results within your company. In the same way, our life plans don't matter much until we start carrying them out. As we execute our life plans, we will realize where we need to make adjustments and changes. Don't be afraid to make the necessary adjustments along the way. Your goal doesn't have to change, however, how you get to that goal may require some adjustments. Don't allow changes to make you forfeit your business, life, and career goals.

#14 Increase Your Productivity | Excellence

There is a difference between being busy and being productive. As you are training to become a gold medalist of life, challenge yourself to increase your productivity. Trim the fat off your day by assessing. Are you spending too much time on social media or surfing the web? Do you spend too much time hanging out with friends? Could this time be used better by resting, fueling your mind, or training your body?

#15 Fuel Your Body | Knowledge is Key

Your diet is the most important aspect of your life. It makes the biggest impact on your performance. A well-rounded diet will allow you to run faster and longer. In the same way, what you consume mentally, the books, magazines, articles, and social media posts you read, impact the competitive advantage you'll have in life. In school, I wanted to know more than any of the other students in the classroom. It was my mission to know more, do more, and outperform my competition, whether in the classroom or on the track. To do this, I had to fuel my mind and my body with healthy things. If you want to be the success story everyone talks about, it starts with a healthy diet.

MARATHON OF LIFE

After college, I needed something to keep me in shape. I explored marathon races around my city and surrounding states. As a retired sprinter, marathons were tough for me. I would always want to sprint out in front of the race and just pace myself in front of everyone else. It soon hit me that I was running someone else's race and that this was not a sprint, but a paced marathon. I began to use this same outlook on life.

Sometimes, we have great ideas, and we want to run with them instead of taking the necessary time to plan before we execute them. Sprinting in life is a one-way ticket to failure and wasting precious time and resources. When you sprint during a marathon race, you burn out quickly, and everyone will eventually pass by you. The difference between life and a marathon is that you are your competition. If you want to stay ahead and on top of your goals, you must begin to see life as a marathon instead of a sprint. As you run your life race, things will happen along the way. Life hits, exhaustion

THE MISSION PLAN: THE DESTINY

creeps in, soreness takes over, distractions surface, and you may even trip up as you cross new terrains. However, you must find the inner strength and dedication to push forward and finish strong. There will be moments when you may want to trot slowly. You may even stop running and begin to walk. But, whatever you do, don't stop running. Use the 15 steps above, stay diligent, and keep your eyes straight. If you stay the course, you will soon find yourself standing on the podium receiving the gold medal.

Pull out your notebook or journal and answer the following questions.

1. What is your definition of success?
2. What do you want out of life? What is your desired best outcome?
3. How much can you balance on a daily?
4. Out of all the things you desire, what do you actually need?

THE MISSION PLAN: THE DESTINY

TIPS FOR SUCCESS

Success is a process and lifestyle of small steps of hard work that position us to finish strong.

If you want to stay ahead and on top of your goals, you must begin to see life as a marathon instead of a sprint.

You can't expect to make a difference in yourself or the world if you can't adjust to the culture.

CHAPTER FOUR

THE FIGHT, THE HIKE, & THE LIGHT

Anyone can enjoy the beauty and benefits of success, but one must first personally define and recognize what success means to them. I teach people that dreams are not built overnight. You can't work hard on Monday and expect to be successful on Tuesday. Success is a process; it happens in stages. As you sharpen your skills, you advance. Every level of success increases in difficulty. I compare this to many of the video games we played growing up. In 1994 Namco created, developed, and published a fighting video game called Tekken. Much like life, in a game of Tekken, every fight and battle we win gets us closer to the long-term goal of winning the war of success or simply moving to the next level. Our daily opponents are society, stereotypes, and systemic stigmas that try to attack your actions, decisions, and livelihood. Every day, we face the same obstacles, are forced to do things, and must choose to adapt to change to consistently win on our quest towards success. Each time

THE MISSION PLAN: THE DESTINY

we are punched in a match, fall, or even get to the brink of destruction and loss, it is up to us to learn the keys, codes, and skills that will equip us with the necessary foundation to get to the next level and unlock hidden talents that are locked inside us. As we fight battles in the war of success, fulfillment, or even peace, we must learn new tricks and knowledge and leverage our experiences from previous rounds. Every level we face prepares us for the moment when we meet the "Final Bosses" or the climax of our success or failure.

Have you ever gone on a hike? Maybe in the mountains or on a hiking trail in your area? The first time I went hiking was during an internship with The United States Department of Agriculture in Fort Collins, Colorado. My boss would always tell me how beautiful the trails were and how difficult it would be to get to the top. I was a track athlete at the time and willing to take on the challenge. We hiked Medicine Bow Peak, which had heights of 12,013 feet high. It is almost the highest mountain in southern Wyoming. Compared to the other mountains in the region, Medicine Bow Peak was small, but the alpine scenery was breathtaking and filled me with peace and fulfillment. The ride there took about three hours, so it gave us time to talk about the journey ahead, sports stories, and where I was aspiring to go in life. As we got closer, I began to feel butterflies at the bottom of my stomach. We arrived early that morning, and I remember the feeling that went through my body as we sat in the parking lot. As we were getting our hiking gear, I looked at the peak of the mountain. My youthful eagerness soon turned into fear and doubt, and I began to question if I even wanted to hike anymore. This internal feeling must have shown all over my face. My boss touched me on my shoulder and asked if I were okay. I nodded my head yes, smiled faintly, and decided to take the challenge.

Sometimes the things we look forward to the most invoke fear within us. When we are face to face with our goals, dreams, and aspirations, the first challenge we face is the fear of taking the first step. That internal feeling shows in our actions, habits, and daily performance. Many of us have gotten so accustomed to it that we don't recognize it. That's why it is important to have people in our lives who will ask, "Are you okay?" Do you have accountability partners willing to put their hand on your shoulder and walk with you towards the peak of your destiny?

That question from my boss served as more than words; it affirmed that he had my back. Not just on the hike, but during my time as an intern at his company. Can you honestly say that your associates, friends, and partners have your back? When you need it most, who's there to help you use your frustrations to fuel your future? Or, do those around you allow you to use your obstacles as a reason to give up?

That sunny day in Wyoming taught me so much. As we climbed 12,000 feet into the sky, I thought about how much my life and the journey ahead of me mirrored our hike. I'd come so far, overcome so many hills, and obstacles, but there was yet more ahead. However, amid the challenge, the scenery around me was so beautiful, I wanted to see what it would look like from a higher altitude. Making it to the peak of the mountain was amazing. The view was beautiful. I imagined that how I felt at that very moment would be the same feeling I would experience as I climbed the mountain of success in my career and personal life. I can recall how I felt standing at the base of the mountain. I couldn't see the peak because clouds covered it, so I visualized what it looked like and how I would feel once I made it to the top. What I imagined was nothing compared to what it actually looked like and how accomplished I felt. Once we begin our journey to success, we see where we want to go, we imagine the beauty in the scenery, but sometimes the peak is hidden by the clouds. At the bottom of the mountain of success, we are well-rested, full of energy, and eager to run to the mountain's top. We even point at the top and say to ourselves, "That is where I am going, and nothing will stop me from getting there. We can't always see the peak, but we can't allow that to stop us from putting on our gear, slathering on the sunblock, unrolling the map, and trekking ahead on to our desired destination.

As we climbed the mountain, there were many times that we stopped, caught our breath, and even considered turning around. Naturally, we could see the rocks from the base of the mountain, and we could safely assume there would be wildlife along the way up. Despite how aware and prepared we were, the reality of the bumps, humps, rocks, snakes, and other wildlife along the trail were sometimes tough obstacles to go through. Even though we had a plan and a map, we still feared being lost or something negative happening. We passed, met, and walked with many people. Someone continued ahead of us, some turned around before they made it to the peak, and some headed back to the base after successfully making it to the top.

In your life, there will be many times when you need to stop and catch your breath. There will even be moments when you will want to turn around and go back to old habits and dead relationships. There will be many bumps, obstacles, humps, trials, tribulations, and yes, even snakes along your journey. You will be challenged to face fear. You will get lost. You will lose people who started with you, be left behind, and even run into those who decided to turn around as you hike to the top. You will have moments when you stop, marvel at how far you've come, and take in the scenery around you. Whatever you do, no matter how high you go, or what obstacles you may face, don't stop. You can only fail if you stop. Success requires resiliency.

LOOK, REACH, & TOUCH THE STARS

Losing my first job after college was a blessing in disguise. Throughout my eight months as an employee, I fought internally between going after my passion or enjoying the perks of a potentially highly profitable profession. I looked at every workday, meeting, and training as an opportunity to build my skillset. I took every lesson I learned and taught the students I worked with outside of work. Having a son before I graduated college left me in a tough position. I wanted to follow my passion, but I also knew I needed to pay my son's $1,200 daycare bill, purchase all his essentials such as diapers, wipes, and formula, and send his mother funds to take care of the things she needed. Any parent reading this knows how expensive it is to raise a child. When I lost my job, the first thought that went through my head was, "How will I pay the daycare bill on Monday?" I wasn't concerned about my outstanding $20,000 credit card debt that I was making monthly payments on. I didn't think about the $35,000.00 student loan debt I had committed to paying on monthly. I didn't think about the $4,000 legal services bill due to the lawyer working with my organization. As a parent, I understood that my sole responsibility as a father was to ensure that my child was taken care of, had shelter over his head, food in his belly, and efficient childcare as his mother worked and went to school. On the day I was fired, I didn't have a dime in my savings. I had the bare minimum in my checking and zero investments to pull from.

For the first time in my life, I didn't have my stuff together. I put all my eggs in one basket, and when that basket was snatched from me, I lost all the eggs in it. I felt useless to the world. On top of the lack of financial stability and confidence, I was without transportation mode because I lost my company car. I remember sitting in the living room in my parent's home and watching my son play with his toys. I closed my eyes and did the only thing I knew to do. I prayed. I was at an ultimate low. I didn't have a "pot to piss in or a window to throw it out of." I needed answers. When I opened my eyes, my son was standing in front of me, smiling with drool coming down his chin, his play telephone ringing in his hand, and a shirt full of food and juice stains. He opened his arms to hug me, and my heart was instantly warmed. At that moment, I realized that though I was down to nothing financially, I was blessed. As I held on to my son, I gained the motivation to believe in myself again. If I didn't do it for myself, I had to do it for him.

When we make our dreams and goals, we don't always anticipate being knocked down, losing our jobs, losing loved ones, or heartbreak. We don't think that at any moment, natural disasters can take our homes, disease can plague our communities, or that new legislation could suddenly change our standards of living. However, these things are real, they happen to people around us, and they can happen to us. Do you want to know what helped me through my difficult season? Well, it's the same thing that allowed me to climb that mountain in Wyoming. Faith. I believe that faith is complete trust, belief, or confidence in something or someone. You can build a new house, buy a new car, meet a new spouse, and even get hired for another job, but faith is an internal belief that no matter what happens, what occurs, or what obstacles are thrown at you, you will make it through, and things will get better.

A life without faith in something or someone is a life not worth living. Faith is unbeatable and untouchable. Faith fuels the woman who bears her first child after being told by doctors that she would never have children. Faith fuels the solider bombed in Vietnam but still lives to tell the stories to his family. Faith fuels the son who has a tragic car wreck, is paralyzed from the waist down, but one day learns how to again. Faith fueled the Civil Rights Movement in America that, through years of oppression and cultural enslavement, brought about change and equality. Faith fueled me, a 24-year-old man, who was down to nothing, to turn my life around in a year. Because of faith, I went from not knowing what was next in my life to speaking to millions around the nation as an author of multiple published books. When we believe in something and are confident about it, we learn that nothing is impossible no matter the challenges we face.

I remember growing up and listening to The Notorious B.I.G.'s hit record in the 90s, "Sky's the Limit." In this song,

THE MISSION PLAN: THE DESTINY

Biggie expresses how he felt when his mother encouraged him to follow his dreams, the hard times in his life, and how his inner confidence and beliefs pushed him forward. Every lyric in this song spoke to me, but the hook resonated with me most.

> *Sky is the limit, and you know that you keep on*
> *Just keep on pressing on*
> *Sky is the limit, and you know that you can have*
> *What you want, be what you want*
> *Sky is the limit, and you know that you keep on*
> *Just keep on pressing on*
> *Sky is the limit, and you know that you can have*
> *What you want, be what you want*
> *Have what you want, be what you want*

These lyrics show what happens if we remain faithful and continue to have hope in a better future. When I got older, I was introduced to a quote by Paul Brandt. It says, "Don't tell me the sky is the limit when there are already footsteps on the moon." Stop putting limits around your life. Stop letting the stereotypical views dictate your decisions. Stop letting people distract you from your destiny. Free yourself from the mental imprisonment of your thoughts.

As we close this chapter, I want to encourage you again to pinpoint what you define as success and go after it. Sometimes, we don't know how to live within our reality because we are so focused on society's dreams. Society makes us believe that we have to graduate from college, work at a Fortune 500 Company, own a mansion, fly in private jets, and make millions of dollars to be successful. If you truly desire these things, that's perfectly fine. However, be careful not to allow your dreams to be contaminated by what the world defines as success. What do you define as success? What is it that you truly desire? What is it that you want in your life? We can become so focused on building our portfolio that we lose the importance of building our character. We are so focused on materialistic inheritances that we forget about building the legacies and learning the lessons we need to pass down to our children. We put so much attention on the present moment that we forget to plan for the future. Set yourself free from the lies, insecurities, criticisms, stereotypes, opinions, and your fears. Pull out your shovel and pave your way to your success.

THE MISSION PLAN: THE DESTINY

The purpose of this challenge is to help you redefine what fuels you. Answer these questions honestly.

1. What do you have faith you can do?
2. What pushes you to go hard each day?
3. What legacies and lessons will you leave to your future children?
4. If money wasn't an issue, what would you do for the rest of your life and why?
5. What will you contribute to the world?

TIPS FOR SUCCESS

Every day, we face the same obstacles, are forced to do things, and must choose to adapt to change to consistently win on our quest towards success.

Whatever you do, no matter how high you go, or what obstacles you may face, don't stop. You can only fail if you stop. Success requires resiliency.

Be careful not to allow your dreams to be contaminated by what the world defines as success.

"As we look ahead into the next century, leaders will be those who empower others."

-Bill Gates

CHAPTER FIVE

IPO: WELCOME TO THE LIFE MARKET

What would life be if the stock market didn't exist? What if we didn't get daily notifications on our smartphones about the Dow Jones or new companies are looking to file an Initial Public Offering (IPO) soon? What would a day without trading, investing, and Wall Street look like? What would this mean for our global economy? If the New York Stock Exchange Board of Directors decided to close shop today, what would happen to the world? In the article, What if the Stock Market Didn't Exist? What would be Different Without the Stock Market, Peter Leeds sets the tone in describing a world without the stock market in terms of global economics. He says, "Many of our biggest and most important corporations got their start by raising millions in the Initial Public Offering stage of their lifecycle." Besides the business economic reasoning, what would the world be without these big corporations, IPOs, and the New York Stock Exchange? What value does the stock exchange hold? How does the stock market impact our society, decision making, and livelihood? Now everyone can't relate to business and global economics, so I want to pose this question... What would life be without you? How does your value or investment impact the lives of those around you?

I read an article entitled, "The Cost of a Human Life, Statistically Speaking: Is there any satisfactory method for assessing the true cost of a human life?" The author of the article, Frank Partnoy, wrote that on July 21, 2012, the U.S. Office of Management and Budget put a value on the human life of $7 million to $9 million. The article explained the factors they based the findings on and what went into the economists coming to this number. He said that economists estimated the value of human life based on the choices we make, such as smoking cigarettes, driving cars, eating undercooked meat, and or working stressful jobs. He explained further how different governmental agencies concluded their findings. In the stock market, we use clear and concise ways to value a stock price or company, but in life, what clear and concise methods are we using to determine the price of a life and its value?

THE FIVE BASIC ELEMENTS OF LIFE VALUE

According to Andrew Beattie in his article, "The 4 Basic Elements of Stock Value," there are four basic elements that investors use to break down a stock's value. Throughout the article, it listed four ratios and what they can tell you about a stock. But in life, what ratios can tell you about a person's stock? How are you valuing yourself after you have entered the life market?

Price to Book Ratio (P/B)
Your Product

In business, the price to book ratio represents the company's value if it's torn up and sold today. In this ratio, the book value includes equipment, buildings, land, and anything else that can be sold, including stock holdings and bonds. Think about this. If you were torn up and sold today, how much would you be worth? If you were to get that offer from that company, accepted into that college, or the investment from that donor, what would it be worth to the party on the giving end? What have you accomplished, and in what way have you contributed to society? How have you impacted the world, country, state, city, or town that you work in? What do you bring to the table?

Often, we want something for our efforts, instead of truly understanding what we have to offer to others. It is not about just gaining knowledge, meeting connections, and getting people to invest in you. What is your overall investment worth?

Price to Earnings Ratio (P/E)
Put Your Money Where Your Mouth Is

The price to earnings ratio is often the most highly scrutinized ratio of them all. Many stocks may suddenly increase because of an event or a new product launches and spikes in stock price. But the P/E ratio is what decides if it can stay up. Because a stock price's increase or decrease is predicated around investors' hopes for earnings, a stock will eventually fall back down without earnings to back up the price. Are you over-promising and under-delivering? Have you oversold your dreams or what you said you were going to do and never lived up to what you said? Have you ever sold people on the idea of a product, and the product was never created? In gambling, people say, "put your money where your mouth is." But in terms of life, let your performance speak for itself. Over centuries in business, there has been so much money and resources put into a product that has never materialized to be as awesome as the marketers thought it would be. Companies have gone bankrupt, doors shut, and workforces fired because of over-promising and under-delivering. In life, let your performance speak for itself. It is not all about what you say. It is about what people or, in business terms, what your consumer sees.

The PEG Ratio
Change = Growth

Instead of just looking at the numbers and price, the PEG ratio incorporates all factors, as well as the historical growth rate of the company's earnings over a period. It also tells you how this stock stacks up against other stocks. The lower the PEG ratio, the better deal you're getting for the stock's future estimated earnings. In business, I believe this is one of the most important ratios that is looked at. Understanding performance trends is very important to understand where the future of a company or your life is going. It is not about just looking at the accomplishments, the trophies, the points where you may have gotten a bonus at work, or some recognition in a press release. It isn't about just graduating from that university or getting promoted at work. Where have you consistently been successful? Where have your consistencies fallen short?

Over the years, what strengths over the years have made you successful? What weaknesses or flaws have been exploited? Again, the only thing constant in life is change. Where there is no change, there is no growth. To consistently grow forward, you must consistently change forward.

Dividend Yield
ROI

The dividend yield is that back up when a stock's growth falls at a given time. This is what is attractive to most investors because it is the interest on our money. This shows the payday that you are getting for your money. What is the return on the investment people, companies, or investors invest in you? Is it a product? Is it the ability to leverage your network? Is it power? Is it knowledge, resources, or just a genuine friendship? How are people going to get paid for how they invest in you? Is what you have to offer to people attractive? Why should they buy what you are selling? Why should they buy your books? Why should they purchase your products? Why should they listen to your words? This is part of building a successful brand as a person. This is more purpose-filled than profit filled. Why you? Why do you matter? At a point in my life, I had a hard time answering these questions. When I was writing the Mission Plan series, my parents would ask me, "Why should people buy your book? What would make someone purchase your book if they don't know you?" Their questions were harsh but very valid and deserving of answers. When mastering these questions, you will become even more attractive to your consumers, investors, and networks. They will soon see the payday that they will be getting for the time,

THE MISSION PLAN: THE DESTINY

The purpose of this challenge is to help you redefine what fuels you. Answer these questions honestly.

Think about the explanations given in this chapter about each of the following. In your journal write how you would describe your life's:
1. Price to Book Ratio
2. Price to Earnings Ratio
3. PEG Ratio
4. Dividend Yield
5. Bottom Line

TIPS FOR SUCCESS

In life, let your performance speak for itself. It is not all about what you say. It is about what people or, in business terms, what your consumer sees.

Where there is no change, there is no growth. To consistently grow forward, you must consistently change forward.

The true purpose of life is empowering, inspiring, aiding, supporting, and giving back to others that may not have been given the same opportunity as yourself.

ABOUT THE AUTHOR

Kyle S. King is an educational and inspirational leader. Currently serving as the Chief Executive Officer and Founder of Project SHINE Inc., he is committed to advancing underrepresented students through comprehensive educational processes that promote excellence and provides them with the skills and resources to become globally competitive business leaders.

He coined the phrase "You do NOT have to be at an Ivy League School to be an Ivy League Student." starting out with local community mentoring efforts and a unique story, later evolving into rigorous school scholar's programs increasing the intellectual standards of students by breaking the stereotypical boundaries.

King is a frequent speaker at educational institutions, national conferences, business consultant and published author, with a focus in the areas of entrepreneurship, student excellence, innovation, business and economic development, and personal and professional development. Other business experience includes NASA, BMW, United States Department of Agriculture, and Johnson & Johnson Inc.

King brings a powerful combination of business and higher education experience to inspire the next generation of future business leaders to act by maximizing their potential. Holding a B.S., in Finance from Alabama A&M University King is committed to offering innovative programs, workshops and events to enhance student learning through real world exposure and hands on activities.

STAY CONNECTED

Hey Mission Planners,

    Thank you for purchasing The Mission Plan: The Destiny. More importantly, thank you for inspiring me to write it! I am overwhelmed with gratitude, joy, and wholeness. I look forward to connecting with you and keeping you updated on my next releases. Stay tuned! There's so much more I am inspired to share with you.

With love,

Kyle

FACEBOOK   Kyle S. King
INSTAGRAM   kylesking
YOUTUBE   Kyle S. King
WEBSITE   kylesking.com
    shineonline.education
    theshineinstitute.com
    blueprintconferences.com

www.ingramcontent.com/pod-product-compliance
Lightning Source LLC
Chambersburg PA
CBHW070617160426
43194CB00009B/1290